HERO
IN THE
FOOTNOTES

*The Life and Times of Richard Cadman
Etches: Entrepreneur and British Spy*

MICHAEL ETCHES

authorHOUSE®

AuthorHouse™ UK
1663 Liberty Drive
Bloomington, IN 47403 USA
www.authorhouse.co.uk
Phone: UK TFN: 0800 0148641 (Toll Free inside the UK)
*   UK Local: 02036 956322 (+44 20 3695 6322 from outside the UK)*

Published by AuthorHouse 03/12/2021

ISBN: 978-1-6655-8457-9 (sc)
ISBN: 978-1-6655-8458-6 (hc)
ISBN: 978-1-6655-8456-2 (e)

Print information available on the last page.

This book is printed on acid-free paper.

Cover Image: London Bridge from The Old Swan by Herbert Pugh (c.1735-1788). Accession 0366, Bank of England. Image © Bank of England.

CONTENTS

PREFACE

Towards the end of 2003, long before I had considered researching my family history, I read a book about the quest for the North-West Passage. It was called *Voyages of Delusion*, by Glyn Williams. As I marvelled at the exploits of Captain James Cook, Christopher Middleton, William Moor, and Francis Smith, I mused to myself that I had never come across anybody intrepid or famous who bore the surname Etches. But a few chapters on, I was amazed to see reference to not just one Etches but two! They were Richard Cadman Etches and his brother John, two entrepreneurs who had formed the King George's Sound Company to trade in sea otter furs off the Northwest Coast of the United States.

Naturally, my first inclination was to try to discover whether the brothers were ancestors of mine. I made a few forays, including a visit to the Natural History Museum in London. There I met Neil Chambers, who was editing the letters of Joseph Banks, a friend of Richard. Neil was aware that there had been correspondence between the two. He gave me the name of Martha Whittaker of the Sutro Library, San Francisco, where a significant amount of Joseph Banks's correspondence and papers are kept. Neil felt that here might be a useful starting point to discover more information about Richard.

But my busy work life as an insurance broker in the City of London, and my family life with teenage sons, somehow distracted me from my quest. It was not until seven years later, when family records became more accessible via online genealogy websites, that I became interested in researching my immediate forebears, but it looked as though any connection with Richard Cadman Etches was remote as I had traced my ancestors to the Worcestershire area, whereas his had come from Ashbourne in Derbyshire.

Eventually, in common with many researchers, I hit the legendary "brick wall" and decided to employ a professional genealogist to help me. She found Etches family records that had not yet been put online.

Suddenly I was looking at ancestors of mine who lived in Ashbourne. In fact, many people bearing the surname of Etches had been born in that town and its environs.

Although Richard was born in Shipston-on-Stour, Warwickshire, his family A moved to Ashbourne probably around 1760, where his father, William, who was a wine merchant, established premises in the marketplace.

With a lot of patience and the assistance of other online researchers who also belong to the Etches family, I have been able to trace my branch back to the point where it links in with his.

Richard Cadman Etches, I believe, is my third cousin, five times removed.

This is his story.

INTRODUCTION

Virtually everything that is known about Richard Cadman Etches's life emanates from a book called *The History and Topography of Ashbourn*, published 20 June 1839 by Dawson and Hobson. The Preface of the book states that it is "an attempt to illustrate in a popular manner the history and topography of that highly beautiful and diversified tract of country, the Valley of the Dove; of which, from its locality, the town of Ashbourn may be said to form a central point". The book appears not to have a single author but rather several anonymous contributors. Its contents are said to have been originally published "in a periodical form", and the success of this venture presumably led to the public demand for a reprint as a book.

The memoirs of Richard Cadman Etches, who had spent part of his early life in Ashbourne, take up the whole of Chapter 4. The publishers show obvious delight in his inclusion and make special mention of him in the Preface:

> One portion of this work, from the attention it has excited, seems to require a passing allusion, that is, the memoir of Mr. Richard Cadman Etches. Had the career of that enterprising individual been less extraordinary, and his services to the country less important, it would have been needless for the compilers to assert, that they believe every tittle of this narrative to be literally and strictly correct; that no fact is exaggerated and that the testimony of his contemporaries will confirm a statement derived from clear and incontrovertible documentary evidence.

If all the events described in Richard Etches's memoirs are "literally and strictly correct", then he had indeed led an exciting and fulfilling life, one that has been sorely neglected by biographers and historians alike.

A review of the book contained in *The Gentleman's Magazine*, volume

12, page 507, published in 1839, summarises the achievements detailed in the book, but it adds the following:

> Mr. Etches appears to have been honoured with the confidence of the government to a high degree, during the time when his utility was felt; but in common with many other political characters, may have been forgotten when his services were less needed.

I was very keen to prove the authenticity of his memoirs—or otherwise—and, if they were true, to determine why the exploits of Richard Cadman Etches were not more widely known. What kind of man was he?

As the oldest son of a successful wine merchant and saddler in Ashbourne, Richard had a reasonable start to life. I like to think of him as entrepreneurial and ambitious from an early age. He came to London to seek fortune and success, both of which he did indeed find. But he was also possessed of a sense of adventure. Had this, coupled with his contacts in high places, steered him into becoming a British spy? His initial business as a wine, spirits, and tea merchant meant that he needed to travel to Europe extensively. Was he therefore a prime candidate for a career in espionage? Until recently, it was thought that he was the inspiration for Baroness Orczy's *The Scarlet Pimpernel*. She was supposed to have visited Ashbourne in 1901 to research her first novel, which was published four years later.

What happened to Richard later in life, though? Why did he end up in a debtors' prison? He banked at Messrs Hammersley, which was founded in 1796 at 76 Pall Mall, but following the death of Hugh Hammersley, the last surviving partner, it was taken over by Coutts & Co. No records of Richard's bank account were found, but Charles E. Etches, who began to compile details of Richard's life in 1950, wrote to the Bank of England about the possible existence of one. He received a letter from the chief cashier dated 19 June 1951, which said:

> There is a joint account, RCE [Richard Cadman Etches] is one of the constituents. The account has remained dormant since 1788 and has a balance of less than 10 shillings.

The letter added a warning that the cost of proving entitlement would vastly outweigh the proceeds!

It seems a great pity that a man who was once described by the MP Nicholas Vansittart as "the most active and intelligent adventurer I have ever met with" should end his days as a debtor in Fleet Prison.

Had Richard chosen a military or naval career instead of becoming an intelligence agent, his name might have been more prominent in the annals of British history.

I discovered that Richard's life could be divided into two distinct halves. One half was spent as an entrepreneur who seized the opportunity to trade in sea otter furs on the Northwest Coast of the United States, and the other half was spent as a British government agent who was active during both the French Revolution and the Napoleonic Wars that followed. Yet despite all this, or perhaps because of it, his name is virtually unknown, and his exploits have been forgotten. I am not aware that any biography of Richard Etches has ever been published. When researching him, I counted myself lucky to find any mention of his name, and when I did, it often appeared only in the footnotes.

Hence the title of *Hero in the Footnotes*.

CHAPTER 1

EARLY DAYS

Members of the Etches family have inhabited Ashbourne for generations. At the time of Richard's birth, it was a small, ancient market town situated on the main London-to-Manchester route close to the point where it crosses the River Dove at a place called Hanging Bridge on the Derbyshire-Staffordshire border. Its proximity to the southern tip of the Peak District mountain chain made Ashbourne a market and service centre for the Dove Valley villages and those of the nearby countryside. Farming was diverse, but the rich surrounding grazing pastures favoured livestock. Eventually Ashbourne became famous for its horse fairs and its cheesemaking. Great quantities of cheese were transported for sale in London. Industrial activity was minimal, apart from several malthouses, the tanneries, and the manufacture of domestic textiles. Despite Daniel Defoe's description of the Peak District as being a "howling wilderness", the area was slowly witnessing the birth of the modern tourist industry with an increasing number of visitors becoming addicted to the cult of the picturesque.

For a small country town, Ashbourne enjoyed an interesting position in English history, mainly involving rebellions by barons against the ruling king of the day. Although Richard left the town as a young man, there are a

Richard was born outside Ashbourne, in Shipston-on-Stour, which lies about eighty-five miles south, but he spent much of his childhood and youth there. In researching my own direct family, I managed to trace ancestors living in Ashbourne in the late sixteenth century. The Etches families are said to have been farming in the area for over five hundred years. I have discovered evidence of their considerable involvement both in horse breeding and cheesemaking.

For a small country town, Ashbourne enjoyed an interesting position in English history, mainly involving rebellions by barons against the ruling king of the day. Although Richard left the town as a young man, there are a couple of historical events which he would have heard about, even if he had not witnessed them, as they both involve members of the Etches family.

The first of these events concerns Charles Edward Stuart, commonly known as the "Young Pretender" or Bonnie Prince Charlie, who, in 1745, marched through Ashbourne on his way to London, where he hoped to enforce the claim of his father, James II, to the crown of England. Charles, supported by the court of France, had been led to believe that as soon as he had set foot on British soil, there would be a general uprising in favour of the Stuart dynasty.

Upon his arrival on Tuesday, 3 December 1745, he billeted himself in Ashbourn Hall. The initial stay was very brief. He and his army soon marched on to Derby. But a few days later, in the absence of reinforcements arriving from France, and perhaps fearing the advance of the king's forces, they returned to Ashbourne, where they caused great disruption to the town and its surroundings. The *Derby Mercury* reported that "some gentlemen's houses were plundered to a great value" and that another man, living in nearby Compton, had been shot dead for refusing to surrender his horse to the rebels.

Leaving Ashbourne, Charles began his retreat northward through Yorkshire to Carlisle. He then led his Highland followers back across the border into Scotland, where they took several towns and seized hold of some important reinforcements. So far, the prince had been fortunate, but on 16 April 1746, his fate was ultimately decided at the Battle of Culloden, where his troops were massacred with dreadful carnage. Disguised as a peasant, he fled. Despite the £30,000 reward for his arrest, nobody betrayed him. He managed to wander through Scotland until he was able to secure a boat, which he took to Roseau, Brittany. With his cause now at an end, he spent the rest of his life on the Continent. He died in Rome in 1788.

In researching Bonnie Prince Charlie's march into Ashbourne, I came across an interesting anecdote in Chapter 3 of *The History and Topography of Ashbourn*:

> A private passing through the market-place, requested a lad to direct him to a shop where he might purchase spirits. The lad accordingly pointed out a spirit shop, the proprietor of

which happened to be standing by at the time. He, fearing the visit of the Highlander, thought proper to deny the fact, and accused the lad of lying. The Highlander, having ascertained that the person did keep a spirit-shop, reported the occurrence to his commanding officer. A court-martial was instituted to inquire into the case, and the spirit-dealer being found guilty, was sentenced to lose his ears. His wife, a beautiful woman, was horror struck at the barbarous sentence. She flew to the Chevalier, and by her tears and urgent entreaties, succeeded in obtaining her husband's pardon.

I cannot know for certain, but it is quite possible that the spirit shop referred to may have been owned by the Etches family in 1745 and could have been the one that William Etches took over. The lucky man who kept his ears intact may have been Richard's grandfather.

Ye Olde Vaults, Ashbourne

The second event concerns James Boswell, who was the companion and biographer of Doctor Samuel Johnson. During their frequent visits to Ashbourne, the two men tended to stay at the home of Doctor John

3

Taylor, a doctor of divinity, who had been a friend of Johnson since their schooldays. In 1776 they were collected from Lichfield and transported in his "large, roomy post-chaise, drawn by four stout, plump horses and driven by two steady jolly postillions". Boswell had a reputation as a ladies' man, but he was distinctly unimpressed with Doctor Taylor's female servants. He wrote in his diary, "None of the Dr's maids were handsome and so I had no incitement to amorous desires." He was more impressed with the landlady at the Green Man public house, a Mrs Killingley, whom he described as "a civil woman who curtseyed very low". He was also impressed on another occasion when he remembered a maid at Ashbourn Hall from previous visits. Her name was Mary Etches. I do not know if she was any direct relation to Richard as the Etches families were quite widespread in Ashbourne by this time.

The Birth of Richard Cadman Etches

I have been unable to find a definitive birthdate for Richard Cadman Etches, but archives at the Warwickshire County Record Office show that he was baptised on 2 November 1753 at Shipston-on-Stour, Warwickshire, almost certainly in the Church of St Edmund. He was the firstborn child William and Elizabeth Etches.

William was living in Shipston and started his family there. As far as is known, his wife, whose maiden name was Elizabeth Cadman, had no connection with Shipston. Probably she was born in Tutbury, Staffordshire, which is where she and William were married on 1 September 1752.

Perhaps William had left Ashbourne to find more lucrative employment in Shipston, which lies about eighty-five miles south. The town's name derives from an Anglo-Saxon word meaning "sheep-wash town". At one time it boasted a thriving sheep market. And because of its location between Stratford-upon-Avon and Oxford, it was also an important stopping place for stagecoaches. Today, many former coaching inns are still to be found in the high street area. There is no indication that William was employed in either of these occupations.

Two more sons were born to William and Elizabeth while they were living in Shipston: William, who was baptised on 8 September 1755, and John, who was baptised on 20 July 1757.

Probably around 1760, William, Elizabeth, and their three sons moved from Shipston to Ashbourne. The couple's next child, a girl named Jane, was born there in 1761 but died within a year of her birth. Three more children were born to the couple: Elizabeth in 1762, Lydia in 1768, and Sarah in 1775. Lydia died at the age of two, but the remaining daughters survived into adulthood.

In Ashbourne, William set up a business as a wine merchant and saddler. His cellars now lie beneath a public house appropriately named Ye Olde Vaults, which is situated in the main town square. On 9 June 1795, at the age of seventy-three, William died. He is buried in the cemetery of St Oswald's Church in a vault, together with his daughters Jane and Lydia.

His will, which was drawn up on 4 June 1795, leaves all his possessions to his wife, Elizabeth; his two daughters Elizabeth and Sarah; and his son John. There is no mention of Richard or William. I wonder if there had been a falling-out between the father and these two sons. As we shall see later, Richard had financial problems towards the end of his life and William was declared bankrupt on 7 November 1793, almost two years before his father's death. The date of Richard's mother's death is unknown.

Little is known of Richard's life in Ashbourne, but as he was the oldest son, it is very likely that he became involved in his father's business. But it was quite common in the late eighteenth century for young enterprising men to want to go to London to seek their fortunes. Richard was no exception.

The City

London was an irresistible lure for the young as it held the promise of work, money, freedom, and excitement or even anonymity and escape. Young men, some with their families, were a common sight as they tramped their way along England's roads in their quest for a better life. The wiser ones made sure that what little money they possessed was sewn into their coat linings as protection against footpads and highwaymen. They left places where the wages were low and moved to places where they could earn more. As the roads and transport improved, mobility and speed improved proportionately.

A Swiss American visitor, Louis Simond, wrote in his book *An American in Regency England*:

> Nobody is provincial in this country. You meet nowhere with those who never were out of their native place, and whose haunts are wholly local. ... To go up to town from 100 or 200 miles distance is a thing done on a sudden, and without previous, deliberation. In France the people of the provinces used to make their will before they undertook such an expedition.

His book was not written until 1810–1811, but the observation was as relevant then as it was a few decades earlier.

The distance from Ashbourne to London Bridge is a fraction under 150 miles. How Richard travelled is not known. Perhaps he could afford to journey by coach, or maybe he walked.

A local historian told me that Richard took his leave from Ashbourne with a friend who bore the surname of Houghton, whose father was the owner of the Green Man. She added that initially Richard wanted to visit other members of the Etches family who had been living in London since the time of the Great Fire in 1666, but I have not been able to find any written evidence of this.

Life in the capital appealed to Richard. He began his career by entering "a large mercantile firm", but his initial ambition was almost certainly to establish a business in London like his father's in Ashbourne, but on a grander scale. By 1775, when he was only twenty-two, Richard and his brother William did just that. As this advertisement in the *Derby Mercury* shows, Richard was still maintaining an interest in the family business despite being resident in London.

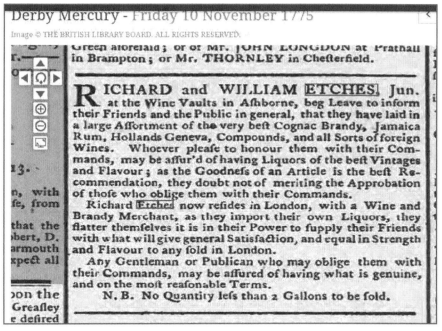

Advertisement from the Derby Mercury

The Dawson and Hobson book states that "in the process of time he became himself the head of an extensive wine establishment", where he imported brandy and tea. His business was initially based in Watling Street and eventually was moved to 38 Fenchurch Street. Records show that his business came under the ward of Langbourn and that he paid income tax of twelve shillings per annum.

Not content with having to buy his stock from importers, Richard had a trading vessel built for his own service and thus was able to trade directly with merchants with whom he had established contact within the ports of France, Holland, and Denmark.

By 1779 he had extended his ambitions by forming a partnership with Robert Hanning Brooks, a tea merchant. The firm was known as "Robert Hanning Brooks, London tea and wine merchants".

Richard had also become apprenticed to the Carpenters' Company. The minutes dated Tuesday, 4 September 1781, of a meeting held at Carpenters' Hall state, "Richard Cadman Etches of Watling Street London Tea Dealer made free by Redemption". He would have been twenty-eight years of age. This means that he had completed his apprenticeship and was now a freeman. Besides being ambitious, Richard possessed an entrepreneurial streak. Membership of the Carpenter's Company would provide an enormous boost to his career.

Originally, in the 1730s, every liveryman had to be a carpenter by trade. This requirement was eventually dispensed with. By the end of the eighteenth century, admittance, either by patrimony or redemption, was being granted to people employed in other trades.

Over time, the typical liveryman in the Carpenter's Company came to be described as someone who was an artisan, sometimes but not always connected to the building trade, who had become wealthy by taking advantage of the opportunities that London had to offer. Earlier in the century, when the French playwright Voltaire visited the city, he noted that commerce had made people freer and that this freedom had allowed them to become wealthier. Here in London, the economic changes had created a new kind of behaviour.

There was lots of new money in Britain, a large portion of it in the hands of a developing class of people who were neither aristocratic nor working class. In his *Letters concerning the English Nation*, Voltaire refers to them as "middlings"—people who now found themselves comfortably off. Perhaps this description fitted Richard. He became a liveryman in 1783, a position he held until his death in 1817.

Although Richard was well on his way to becoming a highly successful businessman in the wine, spirits, and tea trade, once he had become aware of the discoveries made by Captain James Cook on the Northwest Coast of the United States, he became a forerunner in an entirely new venture—as a trader in sea otter furs.

The gravestone of William Etches

CHAPTER 2

THE KING GEORGE'S
SOUND COMPANY

The 11 January 1780 issue of the *London Gazette* contains the announcement of the death of Captain James Cook. This news had arrived eleven months after he and four members of his crew had been murdered by local natives on an Hawaiian beach. It would not be until 4 October 1780 that the two ships he took on his third and final voyage, *Resolution* and *Discovery*, would dock in the Thames after an absence of just over four years.

It would take another four years before Cook's journals were published. Their completion had been left in the hands of James King, Cook's second lieutenant. Because of Cook's untimely death, King had to write the third volume himself. The complete set was eventually handed over to the Admiralty, but the unsettled times that prevailed would delay its publication until the year after the Treaty of Paris, which brought an end to the American Revolutionary War, was signed in 1783.

Nevertheless, very soon after the two ships had returned, word began to circulate the streets of London about the enormous wealth that could be amassed in Canton (China) from the sale of sea otter skins obtained for "trifles" from the native tribes of Nootka Sound on the Northwest Coast of the United States.

Working as a merchant trader in the heart of the City of London, Richard must have been alerted to the exciting prospects that would ensue from this. Now he could begin to formulate plans as to how he could seize the initiative and become a prime mover.

Many of the rumours were confirmed in the official report of Cook's expedition, which was entitled *A Voyage to the Pacific Ocean*. Now, at last, the public were able to examine an enormous amount of reliable and detailed information arising from this three-volume set—information which had been verified by James King's own supportive testimony and views. King had made the following entry in his own journal:

> The advantages that might be derived from a voyage to that part of the American coast, undertaken with commercial views, appear to be of a degree of importance sufficient to call for the attention of the public.

In 1783 James Matra, who had sailed with Joseph Banks, a botanist and naturalist, on Cook's first voyage, had remained friends with him and now sought his backing. Banks had become one of the most influential men in England and was keen to promote the trading ventures that were now being planned in the light of Cook's discoveries.

Matra's proposal involved the establishment of a penal colony in New South Wales. This, he felt, would "atone for the loss of our American colonies" by providing a settlement for loyalists, as well as a base for the development of an extensive trade in the Pacific. Commerce with Canton could be expanded if the Russian trade in the Aleutian Islands could be carried on by ships from New South Wales. Just as Cook's ships had delivered sea otter furs from the North Pacific, so ships from New South Wales could continue the trade and thereby end the current need for British merchants to transport enormous quantities of silver to Canton in exchange for oriental goods.

The contents of Matra's report had soon found their way into open circulation.

As a friend of Banks himself, it is highly likely that Richard knew about the proposal, but now that Cook's official journals had been published, any lingering doubts he may have had about participating in the sea otter trade would have been dispelled. Richard was just one of several entrepreneurs who saw the opportunities, though. He was not the first one to sail forth.

By the end of 1784, several traders, including those based in other parts of the world, had contrived to become the first to take part in this lucrative trade. Back in London, the Court of Directors of the East India Company were viewing these developments with a degree of trepidation because at the present time, by only allowing British ships to operate under their licences, they and the South Sea Company held a monopoly over them.

The fear now was that some British traders would bypass the need for licences by sailing under foreign flags of convenience. The Portuguese flag would be a good example as it would give them permission to trade in Macao, which was a Portuguese port. There was also little the two companies could do about rival traders from foreign parts who might steal trade from them.

They realised early on that they would either need to venture into the trade themselves or form a partnership with other British traders. Despite these fears, the first independent voyage undertaken in the maritime sea otter fur trade seems to have gone ahead with the knowledge of the Court of Directors and perhaps even with their consent.

John Henry Cox and John Reid were trading partners who saw the advantages of being based in Canton and of their connections with India, which they believed could easily be developed into a market for the sale of sea otter furs. With his other associates, including Henry Lane, William Fitzhugh, and David Lance, who were all East India Company supercargoes in Canton trading privately on their own accounts, Cox sponsored a pioneering voyage to be led by James Hanna.

On 15 April 1785, Hanna had set out from Macao in the aptly named vessel *Sea Otter*, arriving in Nootka Sound on 8 August. Despite an unpleasant altercation in which some of the local natives were killed, his venture was successful. He returned to Macao with 560 pelts worth over 20,000 Spanish dollars. News of his success soon found its way into the English press and was fully reported in September 1786.

The success of Hanna's venture led his backers to sponsor a second voyage in 1786. Departing once more from Macao, he arrived in Nootka Sound to discover that he had been preceded by an expedition from Bombay led by James Strange. There is some speculation that Strange may have been representing Richard and possibly acting as an informal adviser to the British government, but I have yet to find evidence of either.

As a result, Hanna was only able to buy fifty skins. He ended up sailing north and charting various islands and inlets. Eventually, in early 1787, he found his way back to Macao, but he died before he could plan a third voyage.

Interestingly, in January 1789, John Henry Cox and Henry Lane would become Richard's business partners in his enterprise called Associated Merchants Trading to the North West Coast of America.

The exact details of Richard's proposed venture have been lost, but his preliminary plans, which were drawn up around March 1785, were ambitious and innovative. His tactic had been to approach the British government with a bold request for a charter which would allow exclusive trade north of latitude 43° 6′ N, plus a settlement at Nootka Sound, a visit to the Sandwich (Hawaiian) Islands, and the development of trade with Japan, which at the time was closed to foreigners.

The government were not prepared to create a charter, but they did give their support to the overall objectives of Richard's undertaking, subject to the approval of the East India Company. In April 1785, Richard forwarded his proposals to their Court of Directors. His comments about Japan were:

> The Japanese Islands would be our grand object to open a
> friendly intercourse with which, we have every possible hope
> of attaining from holding out so great a temptation as the
> Sea Otter skins.

He proposed that the funds from these transactions would be deposited in the East India Company treasury at Canton. He also approached the South Sea Company.

On 4 August 1785, Richard obtained a five-year licence, effective 1 September 1786, from the South Sea Company, and a few days later he was granted a similar one from the East India Company. It had been undoubtedly more difficult for him to achieve this licence, but through his involvement in the tea trade, Richard had connections with the East India Company and was fully familiar with their culture of operation.

Richard's comment below demonstrates not only his knowledge of Cook's final expedition but also his shrewdness. The hydrographer at the East India Company, Alexander Dalrymple, was a great believer in the existence of the North-West Passage—a possible trade route from the Pacific Ocean to the Atlantic Ocean by mean of Arctic waterways—and it is a testament to Richard's artfulness that in his submission to the company he stated:

> There are a number of inlets in Prince William's Sound, and Cook's River, that time would not permit Captain Cook to explore—it is very probable—that some very essential discoveries may be made and perhaps a communication carried on to Hudson's Bay. ... And likewise to make a further attempt to discover a North West Passage.

Although he now had the go-ahead, not a lot was known about the Northwest Coast and its principal destination, Nootka Sound. Cook had only spent a month there on his way to the north, and despite his recognised skill in this field, the maps and charts produced by him and his crew were probably not totally reliable. At this stage it would be worthwhile to look at Cook's experiences along the Northwest Coast more closely.

Captain James Cook

The *London Gazette* referred to earlier also carries an obituary:

> This untimely and ever to be lamented Fate of so intrepid, so able, and so intelligent a Sea-Officer, may justly be considered an irreparable Loss to the Public, as well as to his Family, for in him were united every successful and amiable quality that could adorn his Profession; nor was his singular Modesty less conspicuous than his other Virtues. His successful Experiments to preserve the Healths of his Crews are well known, and his Discoveries will be an everlasting Honour to his Country.

It is difficult to overstate the shock and grief that engulfed everyone as the news spread through the land and the whole nation joined in mourning this great man. King George III had such a high opinion of Cook and was so moved by his death that he shed tears and immediately ordered a pension of £300 per annum for his widow. Using a pseudonym, the botanist and naturalist Joseph Banks wrote a long and flattering tribute in the *Morning Chronicle*.

James Cook was born on 7 November 1728 in the village of Marton, Yorkshire. He began work at the age of sixteen in a grocer's and haberdasher's shop in a fishing village, where it is said that as he gazed out of the shop window, he first experienced the lure of the sea. Proving to be unsuitable for shop work, he left and travelled to Whitby, a nearby port town, where he was taken on as an apprentice working aboard coasters which transported coal from the River Tyne to London. Here he learned mathematics, astronomy, navigation, and charting, subjects at which he soon excelled. At the end of his apprenticeship, he worked on ships in the Baltic Sea, but in June 1755, he decided to join the Royal Navy. This was at the time when Britain was preparing for what became known as the Seven Years War, during which Cook served in North America, where his talents for cartography and surveying brought him to the attention of the Admiralty and the Royal Society.

This led to Cook's appointment as the commander of a scientific voyage to the Pacific Ocean. His main purpose was to observe and record the 1769 transit of Venus across the Sun, but he was also asked to scour the South Pacific for signs of the postulated rich continent of Terra Australis, supposedly a large unexplored land mass situated near the bottom of the Southern Hemisphere. Cook sailed to New Zealand and then to the Polynesian Islands, which he mapped out. Then, continuing westward, he reached the southern coast of Australia. On 28 April 1770, he arrived at Botany Bay, so named because of the many unique plant specimens found there by Joseph Banks, who had travelled with Cook as the official botanist. Returning to England on 12 July 1771, Cook published his journals, and within the scientific community at least, he became something of a hero.

In August 1771, Cook was promoted to the rank of commander. The following year he was commissioned by the Royal Society to lead another expedition to search for the fabled Terra Australis. In 1773, he crossed the Antarctic Circle and explored the region, almost managing to reach mainland Antarctica, but in urgent need of supplies, he was forced to turn eastward. In 1774 he returned to New Zealand before making his way home to Britain. The reports that were published upon his return finally dispelled the myth of Terra Australis. Cook was now showered with honours. He was promoted to post captain and was given an honorary retirement from the Royal Navy, in addition to an appointment as officer of the Greenwich Hospital. He was awarded a medal for completing a voyage without the loss of a single man to scurvy. By now his fame had spread way beyond the bounds of the Admiralty. He was made a fellow of the Royal Society. He had his portrait painted, and he dined with James Boswell. In the House of Lords, he was described as "the first navigator in Europe".

But Cook had accepted his retirement reluctantly. The lure of the sea lingered on, and he insisted that he be allowed to relinquish his position should an opportunity for an active posting in the Royal Navy arise. In 1776, one did. Cook volunteered for his third and, as it turned out, fatal expedition. His mission this time was to find the North-West Passage. He took command of HMS *Resolution*, while Charles Clerke commanded HMS *Discovery*.

As stated earlier, in his submission to the East India Company, Richard Etches had referred to the possibility of the North-West Passage being discovered. For several centuries, European explorers had sought a navigable trade route to the Pacific Ocean through the Arctic Ocean via the waterways of the Canadian Arctic Archipelago. These various islands are separated from each other and from the Canadian mainland by a series of waterways known as the North-West Passage. In ancient times it was known as the Strait of Anián. Many explorers had attempted to locate it without success.

The passage was highly important because, if discovered, it would dramatically improve international trade by allowing ships to journey from the Atlantic to the Pacific and back across northern Canada, thereby avoiding the long and treacherous journey around Cape Horn or the even longer voyage around Africa's Cape of Good Hope. It would also open fresh and lucrative markets along the whole of the Pacific Northwest of the United States.

An Act of Parliament passed in 1745, but now extended in 1775, offered a reward of £20,000 to the first person to discover the passage. The plan was for Cook to travel to the Pacific while another expedition would travel the opposite route from the Atlantic.

Cook departed from Plymouth in July 1776. Having stopped briefly at Tahiti, he travelled north and became the first European to come into contact with the Hawaiian Islands, which he named the Sandwich Islands after the 4th Earl of Sandwich, the acting First Lord of the Admiralty.

In February 1778, continuing his journey across the Pacific, Cook made his way to the Northwest Coast, north of the Spanish settlements in Alta, California. Eventually, in atrocious conditions, he made landfall on the Oregon coast, which he named Cape Foulweather. The bad weather persisted, making it impossible for him to continue northward to search for a North-West Passage. He was eventually driven south. Unknowingly, the ships had, under cover of darkness, sailed past the Strait of Jean de Fuca, which allegedly led into a vast inland sea.

Both vessels were in urgent need of water and substantial repairs, but Cook was unable to make landfall again until 29 March, when two adjacent inlets were sighted. Anchorage was found in a vast bay which Cook named King George's Sound, which was later renamed Nootka Sound by the Admiralty. Almost immediately, Cook and his men came face to face with the local natives, who welcomed them by surrounding their ships with around thirty to forty canoes and shouting at the tops of their voices. They were covered in grease, paint, and dirt, but they were very keen to trade. Cook's men soon discovered that they could barter a ship's nail, a small piece of iron, a buckle, or some ornament of trifling value in exchange for prime sea otter furs.

The repairs needed to the ships meant that Cook was unable to leave Nootka until 26 April. During their stay, he and his men had enjoyed the company of the natives despite their pilfering and their growing demand for more valuable items than trinkets in exchange for the skins. At the time, Cook and his men had little idea of the commercial value of these skins, but they thought them attractive and had no doubt that they would provide warm covering for the Arctic regions into which they were headed. On the day of departure, the chief of the local tribe came aboard *Resolution* and presented Cook with a magnificent beaver skin coat. Cook reciprocated with the gift of a broadsword with a brass hilt.

From Nootka, Cook at last managed to make his way north and map all the coastline as far as the Bering Strait, on the way identifying what became known as Cook Inlet in Alaska, but he consistently failed to sight any evidence of a North-West Passage. Various officers on board, such as William Bligh (later of *Bounty* fame) and George Vancouver, began to think that the existence of a passage was unlikely. The ships pressed on until they reached the limits of the Alaska Peninsula, where they encountered nothing but an impenetrable wall of ice. Frustrated, Cook made his way back to the Bering Strait. By early September 1778, he was ready sail to Hawaii for the winter.

On 17 January 1779, he dropped anchor in a bay known as Kealakekua, where he stayed for a month before deciding to resume his exploration of the northern Pacific. But *Resolution*'s foremast broke, and he was forced back to the bay for repairs. The relationship between Cook's men and the Hawaiians began to sour. Tensions rose and several quarrels erupted. Then, on 14 February, an incident occurred that would have devastating consequences.

Discovering that *Resolution*'s cutter (a small sailing boat) had been stolen from its mooring, Cook retaliated by seizing all the canoes in the bay and confiscating them until the cutter was returned. He told a group of his men to arm themselves and take out boats to block any escape from the harbour. With nine of his marines, he then went ashore, landing at the village of Kaawaola, where he planned to kidnap the old king Terreeoboo and hold him hostage on board *Resolution* until the matter was sorted.

But upon his return to the shore, Cook and his party were gradually surrounded by hundreds of villagers. When news came that a chief who been attempting to leave the bay had been shot, the mob were incensed. One of them threw a rock which struck Cook. Another one threatened him with a knife. One of the marines was attacked, but he beat the aggressor back with the butt of his gun. Cook fired his pistol, but the villagers threw more stones and rocks. Cook fired once again. As he turned his head to shout something to the launch, he was attacked once more. There is some confusion as to whether Cook was stabbed in the neck or shoulder or hit with a club. In any event, he fell forward, into the shallows, and the throng surged around, killing him and four of his men. The others scrambled desperately into the launch and made for safety.

Cook's grieving officers demanded the return of his body, threatening to destroy the village if their demand was not met. A few days later, a piece of Cook's flesh, taken from his buttocks, was delivered. His skull was supposedly in the possession of the old king whom Cook had planned to kidnap. The rest of his corpse was said to have been burned, dismembered, and distributed. Cook's intestines were alleged to have been used to rope off an entrance to the stone temple. I should add that recent research has cast doubts upon the veracity of some of these gruesome details.

Following Cook's death, Charles Clerke took over command of *Resolution* and the expedition returned to the Northwest Coast, but when Clerke, who was already unwell, died of consumption on 22 August 1779, the American John Gore succeeded him. James King was appointed commander of *Discovery*; he remained with her for the rest of the voyage.

Calling at Canton, China, on his way home, King had about twenty pelts in his possession, most of which had been the property of the late Clerke. Going ashore to buy stores and provisions, he found that the skins were highly prized by the Cantonese merchants. He had no difficulty at all in disposing of them for the sum of $800. The officers and men soon picked up on this. One man sold his supply for $120 per pelt.

The Sea Otter

Sea otters (*Enhydra lutris*) are small marine mammals whose habitats are on the coasts of the Northern and Eastern Pacific Ocean. They were prolific along the shores of Alaska, the Pacific Northwest, British Columbia, and California, where the reefs and rocks provided them with protection against the pounding surf and savage storms. They tend to keep close to the nearshores, from where they dive to the seabed to forage. Their diet is mostly sea urchins, worms, molluscs, and crustaceans.

Unfortunately, the sea otters' fearless and friendly disposition towards humankind ultimately led to their downfall. Between 1741 and 1911, they were hunted relentlessly for their fur, with the result that by 1911, the British Columbia population had virtually been wiped out.

Sea otters possess an exceptionally thick coat of fur—in fact, the thickest of the entire animal kingdom. "Strikingly beautiful, the dense, fine underfur with its tipping points of brown and black sprinkled with strands of long silver hair gave a shimmering effect when disturbed by even the slightest breath of air." A male adult pelt could reach a length of five feet and a width of around two and a half feet. When pieced expertly together, the pelts would be made into royal robes for wealthy mandarins. The tails and other oddments could be turned into hats or trim for elaborate gowns.

It has been estimated that between 1790 and 1812, the Cantonese imports from the Northwest Coast averaged twelve thousand skins per year. Sea otter pelts commanded higher prices than any other fur in the Chinese market. In 1779, Cook's men were paid an average of $100 for a complete skin, but six years later, as trade gathered momentum, James Hanna was said to have bettered this by receiving $140 per pelt.

A sea otter

The King George's Sound Company

Richard could now formulate his company. Its full title was the United Company of Merchants, trading to the King George's Sound Company, but very soon it was just referred to either as the King George's Company or the Richard Cadman Etches Company after its "prime mover and principal investor". King George's Sound was the name Captain Cook had given to Nootka Sound. The company had a nominal capital of £200,000 with shares of £100 each, but there are reasons to believe that perhaps only a quarter of the money was ever raised.

The nine partners in the syndicate consisted of seven merchants and two seamen, Nathaniel Portlock and George Dixon, who had sailed with Cook. On two occasions, Richard issued slightly different versions of the partners, but those below are common to both lists:

Richard Cadman Etches, merchant of London
John Hanning, gentleman of Dawlish, Devon
William Etches, merchant of Ashbourne, Derbyshire (Richard's father)
Mary Camilla Brook, tea dealer of London
William Etches, merchant of Northampton (Richard's brother)
John Etches, merchant of London (Richard's brother)
Nathaniel Gilmour, merchant of Gosport, Hampshire
Nathaniel Portlock, seaman
George Dixon, seaman

Richard referred to himself as the governor and to his brother William as the deputy governor. He declared that they, together with William Etches, his father, were "the only proprietors of the Capital Stock", amounting to £25,000.

The two seamen were soon appointed captains of the company's first two trading vessels: the *King George* and the *Queen Charlotte*. Having sailed with Cook on his third expedition, both men were familiar with the region. Many of the men who had been with Cook were eager to return to the Northwest Coast. Portlock and Dixon were no exception.

Nathaniel Portlock, born in 1748, probably in Norfolk, Virginia, was a highly experienced sailor. He had entered the Royal Navy in 1772 as an able seaman serving on HMS *St Alban's*. Four years later, he joined HMS *Discovery* as master's mate and served on Cook's third voyage. During the expedition, in August 1779, he transferred to HMS *Resolution*. He passed his lieutenant's examination on 7 September 1780 and then served on HMS *Firebrand* in the Channel Fleet.

George Dixon, who was also born in 1748, served under Cook on HMS *Resolution* as armourer's mate. In 1782 he was engaged by William Bolts, the representative of an Austrian company trading to Asia. Bolts's plan was to send a ship, *Count Cobenzell*, from Trieste to the Northwest Coast. But according to Dixon's later account, the expedition which "was so exceedingly promising in every point of view, was overcome by a set of interested men, then in power in Vienna". This, coupled with insufficient funds, brought a premature end to the venture.

Dixon returned to England and approached Sir Joseph Banks and several English traders, of whom it is to be assumed Richard was one, about participation in the sea otter trade. These discussions culminated in the formation of the King George's Sound Company. Dixon became a partner.

Richard had appointed Portlock to take overall command, and William Beresford, a trader who sailed on the *Queen Charlotte*, had been employed to keep a detailed record of the journey. Portlock had been told to call at Cape Horn, where he was to leave supplies for other ships to follow. He also had instructions to establish a colony at Nootka Sound and to build a factory and housing accommodation there.

In an identical letter dated 3 September 1785, which was given to both Portlock and Dixon, Richard set out his detailed instructions:

On your arrival at the North West coast you are to make the first convenient port you can endeavour to cultivate friendship with the natives for the purpose of trade using items to barter and to give presents.

You are required to traffic with them with that liberality, integrity and generosity as shall imprint on their minds the true character of a British merchant.

Although furs are the main item of traffic you are to enquire, particularly at King George's Sound, about copper, and whatever other articles of commerce there are to be met with and for future trade you are to establish such factories as you shall see necessary and confident with the safety of such settlers, and your ship's company King George's Sound looks the most ideal but you must use your discretion. You are to purchase a tract of land from the natives as you see best suited for trading and security paying them in the most liberal and friendly manner for the same.

You are to give them [settlers and factory hands] every assistance to erect a log house and/or such other buildings as shall appear necessary for their residence and for carrying on a traffic with the natives.

You are to leave them such quantities of provisions and other articles of convenience, for the purpose of carrying on a trade.

Always have our motto in your mind "Commercio liberali crescimus"

[By trade we prosper].

You are particularly ordered while you remain at the cape or any other place you touch at, to refresh your ship's companies, before entering the Pacific Ocean and to put your vessels in the best possible state of defence. That you keep proper discipline among your people [crew] and wherever you touch to act with the utmost prudence and caution.

On your arrival at Canton, should the ships be ordered to Europe on the East India Company's account and you have established any factories in the course of your voyage you are to, in that case, purchase a vessel to return to the said factories.

You are also requested to take a draft or sketch of any place you may discover and if such ports have not before been visited by other nations you are to take possession with the consent of the natives, which you will attempt to gain by making them presents (the light horsemen's caps will be a good emblem of your having been among them) in the name of the King of Great Britain; and set up such marks and inscriptions as you will give testimony of such parts having been taken possession of by His Majesty's subjects.

PS: I have omitted to mention that you are particularly required not to let slip any possible opportunity of sending intelligence of your proceedings from the time you leave the English Channel until your return to England; you are to address such dispatches to Richard Cadman Etches, London and enclose them, under cover, to George Rose Esq., at The treasury, London.

Nathaniel Portlock

CHAPTER 3

RICHARD'S FIRST
NORTHWEST COAST
VENTURE

The two merchant vessels that Richard had managed to secure departed from Deptford dock on 29 August 1785. Sir Joseph Banks and George Rose, the secretary of the Treasury, were present to christen them. The 320-ton *King George* had a crew of fifty-nine, and the 200-ton *Queen Charlotte* had a crew of thirty-three. The vessels, having been extensively stocked with trade goods and "implements of husbandry", sailed off amid an atmosphere of great expectation.

A report in a local newspaper stated that there was "every probability the present enterprise [would] … open a new source of commercial wealth of the first consequence to this nation".

Both mastheads flew the colours of the King George's Sound Company. They consisted of "the figure of Hope, leaning on an Anchor in an oval, in the center of an Ensign".

Richard and Sir Joseph Banks

It was no surprise that Richard had invited Sir Joseph Banks to christen the *Queen Charlotte*. Banks had given him his support from the beginning, and he had visited the docks to watch the vessels being fitted out. He had also lent Portlock a copy of one of Cook's logs.

Richard's brother John had described Banks as a leading patron of schemes "for prosecuting and converting to national utility the discoveries of the late Captain Cook".

Born on 24 February 1743 in Argyll Street, Soho, the son of a wealthy Lincolnshire squire and member of the House of Commons, Banks had become an internationally respected botanist, naturalist, and patron of the natural sciences. He had sailed with James Cook in HMS *Endeavour* on his first voyage of discovery to the South Pacific from 1768 to 1771. Returning home to England on 12 July 1771, he instantly became famous.

On 30 November 1778, at the age of twenty-three, he was elected president of the Royal Society. Three years later he was made a baronet. During much of this time, he was an informal adviser to King George III on the Royal Botanic Gardens at Kew.

In March 1779 he married Dorothea Hugessen and settled into a large house at 32 Soho Square, London. Here he welcomed scientists, students, authors, and many distinguished foreign visitors. He corresponded with explorers and scientists from all over the world. He also maintained his interest in exploration, especially in Australia because of the time he had spent there with Cook. This led to an interest in the British colonisation of that continent. He was a great proponent of settlement in New South Wales. In 1779, when giving evidence before a committee of the House of Commons, he stated that in his opinion the place most eligible for the reception of convicts "was Botany Bay, on the coast of New Holland [Australia]", on the general grounds that "it was not to be doubted that a Tract of Land such as New Holland, which was larger than the whole of Europe, would furnish Matter of advantageous Return".

Richard was therefore wise to approach Banks, whom Robert M. Galois, in his book *A Voyage to the North West Side of America*, describes as being "positioned at the interface of the highest levels of scientific, political and commercial activity in England" and "a key figure whose support would be invaluable".

Banks was greatly interested in Richard's expedition. The two men had met on 13 March 1785, most likely at 32 Soho Square, where Richard presented his detailed proposals and sought Banks's advice and patronage. Banks appears to have been immediately supportive of Richard's project. Throughout its vicissitudes, he and Richard maintained a correspondence which, as far as can be ascertained, extended over a period of at least seven years, from 1785 to 1792. Unfortunately, only about a dozen letters remain, and these are all from Richard to Banks. It is likely that Banks responded to some or all of Richard's letters, but no record of his replies can be found.

Richard's initial letter was written from his Watling Street premises and was dated 14 March 1785. It begins with Richard thanking Banks for the "high honor done us yesterday by your kind offers of assistance for the matureing [of] our plan", suggesting perhaps that the two had met the previous day and Richard had outlined his proposals to Banks. The letter also speaks of the encouragement Banks had given Richard about "the prospect of opening a friendly Commerce with the Japanese". Richard reasoned that just as sea otter furs were highly valued in China, so would they be in Japan if proffered for sale there. It was rumoured that they would fetch an even higher price in Japan. The problem was that, for a long time, Japan had been refusing to trade with European nations except for Holland, which was allowed limited access to one Japanese port, Dejima, in Nagasaki Bay. With his network of contacts around the world, Banks was the ideal person to obtain reliable information about any relaxation in Japan's attitude. He had "offered to write to his Friend who had made the tour of Japan".

Who this friend was and whether he was able of be of assistance is not recorded, but possibly Banks had in mind the outstanding Swedish botanist and traveller Carl Peter Thunberg, who had stayed in Japan during 1775–76 and had been in recent correspondence with Banks. Banks had also suggested that in addition to the £20,000 Richard had proposed to raise to fit out the two ships, the company needed a much more substantial capital investment. Richard's letter states that he agreed with Banks and was proposing a nominal capital of £200,000, to be divided into shares of £100 each. However it is doubtful whether this amount was ever raised.

Sir Joseph Banks

The Voyage

After leaving Deptford, the first land the two ships made for was the islands of Tenerife. They stayed here for ten days, taking on board more food and water. Then they made for St Jago, Jamaica. Having watered there, they headed for the Falkland Islands, which they reached in January 1786. After sixteen days spent at Port Egmont, the two ships rounded Cape Horn and began their journey north up through the Pacific. On 24 May, they arrived at the island of Hawaii, which was part of what was then known as the Sandwich Islands.

Despite needing fresh fruit and vegetables to combat an outbreak of scurvy, Portlock, having been a member Cook's crew, was wary about the reception that the old chief Kamehameha might give him. So, he remained at anchor in Kealakekua Bay, the place of Cook's death, while trading with the natives for fresh food. Eventually the ships moved on to the other islands: Molokai, Oahu, Kauai, and finally Nihau, where the crews found a good supply of pigs and yams.

On 13 June, the two ships left the islands and headed for Cook's River in Prince William Sound, Alaska, where they attempted to buy sea otter pelts but found them to be in short supply. It was here that they came across some Russian traders. On 13 August, the ships sailed out from Cook Inlet and began to journey south. On 22 September, they reached Nootka Sound but found that they were unable to manoeuvre their ships into the inlet. Eventually they decided to head back to Hawaii for the winter.

It was not until 15 March of the following year that they returned to Alaska and anchored off Montague Island, at the entrance to Prince William Sound. The local Chugach people visited them and repeatedly used the word *Nootka* while pointing to the north-east, but the crews did not understand what the word meant.

Portlock arranged for his ships to be moved into Prince William Sound, where both vessels were hauled up onto a beach for repairs. Dixon was put in charge of the longboats and was sent on an excursion to Snug Corner Cove at the top of the Sound. The local natives told him about another ship from Europe that had spent the winter in the Sound. The natives led Dixon up to Port Fidalgo, where he found the ship *Nootka*; her captain, John Meares; and his crew in an extremely distressed condition.

John Meares

The son of an eminent attorney, John Meares was born in Dublin, probably around 1756. At the age of fifteen, he joined the Royal Navy, serving as cabin boy, before eventually being promoted to midshipman. While serving during the American Revolutionary War, in 1778 he received his commission as lieutenant.

When the war ended with the signing of the Treaty of Paris in 1783, Meares, along with many other officers, found himself with few prospects within the Royal Navy. Now placed on reserve and with his pay reduced by half, he was free to do as he liked. Being possessed of a spirit of adventure, in 1785 he decided to sail to Calcutta to seek his fortune. Meares's first desire was to set up a fur trading enterprise on the Northwest Coast of the United States, which would include a trading post manned by Chinese workers with local natives being enrolled to support it through the supply of pelts. The pelts would be transported by ships and sold in China with stops at the Sandwich (Hawaiian) Islands for "refreshment".

John Meares

Among other things, Meares had been described as "a lovable rogue, full of high-sounding phrases and grand ideas". He therefore had no difficulty in charming several local merchants into joining him in his venture. The partnership was called the Bengal Fur Society. His partners baulked at the thought of paying the ever-exorbitant licencing costs imposed by the East India Company and the South Sea Company, so Meares decided to avoid them by registering his ships in Macao, a Portuguese colony, and by flying the flag of Portugal.

On 20 January 1786, Meares purchased two vessels: the two-hundred-ton *Nootka* and the hundred-ton *Sea Otter*, chosen for their ability to navigate around the inlets and islands of the Northwest Coast. Meares would take charge of the expedition and be the captain of *Nootka*, and William Tipping, a Royal Navy colleague also on reserve and half pay, was appointed as captain of *Sea Otter*.

The two ships set sail at different times but agreed to rendezvous that summer. Meares sailed along the Northwest Coast to trade at Nootka Sound and then in Alaskan waters. But in the Aleutian Islands, his ship was often beset with dense fog and Russian traders prevented him from undertaking any sea otter trade with the natives. He was left with no option but to sail farther north.

A few days later, Meares entered Snug Corner Cove in Prince William Sound. Here he was told that William Tipping had recently left, his ship well stocked with furs. The local native chief, Shenawah, was welcoming, and Meares soon forged a bond with him. He entered into a treaty with the chief under which he promised him gifts if Shenawah would agree to trade exclusively with any of Meares's ships. The chief also built a rudimentary house for the use of Meares's ship's carpenter and his men.

Shenawah promised more furs if Meares continued to stay, but this created a dilemma for him. Meares had arrived too late in the season to acquire the number of pelts he needed and would eagerly accept more. But as far as he was aware, no ship's captain had ever taken the decision to remain in Alaska during its harsh, savage winters, preferring to sail to the Sandwich Islands and enjoy the warmth and comforts they provided.

Meares decided to stay. Moving *Nootka* to a more sheltered and comfortable anchorage, he put his crew to work building a work and trading station. The natives soon began to steal his crew's tools and equipment and made the crew feel intimidated. Deciding to abandon the project, Meares returned his men to the ship. But the natives then besieged the vessel. At one point, Meares was forced to fire a cannon to frighten them off. They soon returned, though, so Meares adopted the new tactic of inviting them on board. Learning that he was interested in sea otter pelts, they offered him trade and were prepared to swap sixty skins for a modest number of "spike nails". But as the weather worsened, the natives retreated to their winter quarters.

It began to snow, and as ice froze around the hull, the men tried to insulate the ship as best as they could, but eventually any work had to be abandoned. For the men to stay warm, fires had to be kept burning all day, but so much smoke was created that they found it almost impossible to breathe. Fresh wood for fuel had to be cut in the nearby forest and laboriously dragged back to the ship. The snow became so deep that hunting for game was impossible. And the salmon had virtually vanished from the streams.

As 1787 arrived, the temperature dropped further and the crew members began to fall ill from the cold, from scurvy, and from the suffocating smoke that enveloped them below decks. Twenty-three reported sick. The snow continued to fall even in April, and men began to die, but at the beginning of May, the weather improved, lifting the men's spirits. The local headman, who had now returned from his winter quarters, informed Meares on 7 May that two ships were at anchor in Prince William Sound. They were the *King George* and the *Queen Charlotte*, newly arrived to start their second season of trading on the Northwest Coast.

The Rescue of John Meares

Meares's crew were overjoyed at the thought of rescue, but Meares was phlegmatic. He said that now that the ice was melting, *Nootka* would almost certainly be able to set sail without any outside assistance. During that terrible winter, twenty-three of his crew had died. Meares later learned that his second ship, *Sea Otter*, had been lost at sea with all hands. The exact number of Tipping's crew is not known, but it was probably around thirty-five. Meares's decision to spend the winter on the Northwest Coast had been a disastrous error in judgement which had resulted in the loss of half his crew and the loss of a ship.

Dixon was both shocked and saddened at the sight of fellow Britons in such distress. He commented that "scurvy had made havock [*sic*] amongst his people … and the remaining part of his crew were so enfeebled … that Captain Meares was the only person on board able to walk the deck". *Nootka*'s men welcomed Dixon as "a guardian angel with tears of joy". Dixon assured Meares that he would provide him with every necessity that he could spare, but from this point onwards, the relationship between the two of them was fraught with controversy.

According to Dixon, Meares told him not to go to the trouble of sending any refreshments to him, because he "would come on board us very shortly in his own boat". Meares partly disputed this by saying that, having already told Dixon of the seriousness of the situation, *Nootka*'s longboat was not seaworthy enough to reach his and Portlock's two ships, which were some "20 leagues away". Dixon's response was that while he could take Meares to the ships, he would not be able to guarantee his return, because Portlock was due to sail very shortly. Meares then addressed a letter to Portlock in which he stressed his own dire condition, that of his men, and that of his ship.

On 9 May, Dixon set sail in his whaleboat, and Meares decided to follow him in his supposedly unseaworthy longboat. He arrived at the *King George* on 11 May, accompanied by his first mate, five seamen, and some supplies of rum and rice, which he hoped to trade for gin, sugar, and cheese. Having refreshed himself, Meares began negotiations with Portlock.

Although Portlock's subsequent account of the proceedings makes no mention of any controversy, Meares, by way of contrast, recorded that Portlock had been less than happy to provide him and his crew with all the supplies they needed. Meares added that Portlock had taken too much credit for his rescue because, by the time Dixon had arrived, *Nootka* was almost certainly able to set sail for the Sandwich Islands. However, he did praise Portlock for providing "considerable assistance and service".

Portlock agreed to supply two of his own sailors to supplement Meares's crew, but only on the condition that Meares pay them £4 per month. Meares considered this to be excessive, especially as, he claimed, Portlock was only paying them 30 shillings per month. Portlock accepted the rum and rice in exchange for brandy, flour, gin, molasses, and sugar. He also instructed his carpenter to caulk the bottom of Meares's longboat. Meares then said farewell and sailed off with the two additional men on board.

A few days later, two whaleboats from the *King George* arrived at *Nootka*'s anchorage. Portlock had written a letter to Meares asking for trading items such as beads, iron objects, a spare anvil, a considerable amount of rice, pepper, and a compass. Meares replied that many of the items were stored deep in *Nootka*'s hold, but he did manage to send the compass, the anvil, and the rice, plus a few other items he thought Portlock might need.

Soon the ice had melted sufficiently for Meares to sail *Nootka* to an anchorage close to the *King George*, which was just inside the Sound and, in honour of Richard, was known as Port Etches. It was now 14 May, and Dixon had left Portlock and sailed south for Nootka Sound. At his next meeting with Meares, Portlock handed him a letter stating that if *Nootka* remained in Prince William Sound to trade with the natives, it would "stop a considerable amount of trade". Portlock therefore made Meares a proposition: if Meares were to pledge a £500 bond never to trade in the area again and also give Portlock twenty bars of iron plus some beads, then Meares could keep the pelts he had already been given. Portlock would then provide "what other assistance I have in my power to give you".

No love was lost between Portlock and Meares, nor between Meares and Dixon. Portlock may have resented the fact that Meares was trading illegally, and even though he had given him assistance, his purpose was to get Meares to leave as quickly as possible because, in effect, he was without a licence, poaching on their grounds. Meares agreed to what he called these "hard conditions … impelled by cruel necessity" but added a few of his own.

He demanded another man, or perhaps a boy, some ale, and other supplies. Portlock agreed to caulk *Nootka*'s deck with oakum and to examine the pumps, but this led to some wrangling between him and Meares over the increasing demands from each side. Eventually, on 18 June, Meares was forced to accept a bond of £1,000 on condition that he sail immediately to Canton. Under protest, Meares agreed. He departed on 22 June.

Portlock's and Dixon's subsequently published journals reveal that both men had some sympathy towards Meares and his plight. Portlock certainly seemed to have done all he reasonably could to help him, and so had Dixon, although he blamed Meares's irresponsibility for creating the high levels of sickness aboard *Nootka* by allowing a "free and unrestrained use of spirits" during the cold weather, especially at Christmastime, when his crew had apparently drunk to excess. Meares denied this, and while he appreciated Portlock's assistance, he maintained that he had given it grudgingly—and had also overcharged him for the supplies.

When Meares left Prince William Sound, his intention was to make for the Sandwich Islands, but poor weather conditions forced him to turn back east. He eventually found refuge near Baranof Island in Alaska's vast Alexander Archipelago.

On 20 October 1787, when he had finally reached Macao, Meares sold his furs. The exact value is uncertain as, despite his pledge to Portlock, he might well have negotiated some trading before he left the coast, but he certainly made enough profit to finance another venture. Meares fully intended to return to the Northwest Coast to trade during the spring and summer of 1788 and to pursue his dream of establishing a permanent trading base there. He had similar views to Richard in that respect, and he was soon to play an important part in his life.

After two years of plying the waters of the Northwest Coast, Portlock and Dixon departed North America and arrived in Macao in November 1787. They had amassed a substantial cargo of furs, but the prices for their sale were disappointing.

While Meares was crossing the Pacific, the *King George* and the *Queen Charlotte* were on their way to Nootka Sound. They had encountered heavy weather during a gale and had been blown off course. The damage was so severe that they were forced to sail to the Sandwich Islands to refit. Having done so and taken on water, they again set sail for Cook's River.

At this point, the two vessels parted company: the *King George* went to trade in the Sound and the adjacent islands, while the *Queen Charlotte* took a more southerly route. Not long after the *Queen Charlotte*'s departure, a party of Indians in canoes drew alongside the *King George*. In their possession, they had some clothes and a belt buckle that had once belonged to a crew member of the *Queen Charlotte*.

Alarmed, thinking that Dixon had encountered some misfortune, Portlock immediately set sail for their intended rendezvous, the Sandwich Islands, leaving behind him a large quantity of half-dried salmon! It was not until he reached Atooi that he heard any further news, and this was in the form of a letter, written by Dixon, which allayed all his fears. It said that Dixon had discovered some islands at which he had been successful in obtaining a full cargo of sea otter skins. He had therefore departed for Macao, naming the islands Queen Charlotte Islands as he left.

Filled with relief at this news, and having a large quantity of skins himself, Portlock set sail the following day for Macao. However, the voyage did not quite end on the high note that he had expected as his goods were sold through the East India Company's supercargoes for a lower sum than he had anticipated: $54,857. Having laded their vessels with tea for the East India Company, Portlock and Dixon sailed for home, arriving in London in August and September 1788 respectively.

Immediately upon his return, Portlock faced Richard's fury because he had failed to carry out a specific duty placed upon him: to establish a fur trading post on the Northwest Coast. But accepting that it would be virtually impossible to persuade men to spend winters in such inhospitable places, he began to form in his mind the idea of possibly colonising the Northwest Coast with convicts.

CHAPTER 4

RICHARD'S SECOND
NORTHWEST COAST
VENTURE

During the two years that Portlock and Dixon were away, Richard had not been idle. Even before he had received any news of their voyage to the Northwest Coast, he had begun to organise a second expedition for the 1787 season. By the time of their return, two additional vessels were trading there. They were:

- the 171-ton *Prince of Wales*, commanded by James Colnett
- the 65-ton *Princess Royal*, commanded by Charles Duncan

James Colnett was a highly experienced mariner. He was born in Devonport, Devon, probably in 1753, but little is known about his early life until 1770, when he joined the Royal Navy as an able-bodied seaman aboard HMS *Hazard*. He then served aboard HMS *Scorpion* as a midshipman under James Cook. In 1771, both men transferred to HMS *Resolution*, and between 1772 and 1775 Colnett served as a midshipman during Cook's second voyage to the Pacific Ocean. Upon his return to England, he continued to serve in the Royal Navy during the American Revolutionary War.

When hostilities ended, in common with most naval officers, Colnett was put on half pay. He had risen through the ranks, eventually being appointed first lieutenant on HMS *Pégase*, but harbour duty in a sedentary role would not have been to his liking after the active life he had so far enjoyed. So, in the summer of 1786, he began negotiations with Richard Cadman Etches & Co. Having obtained approval for a leave of absence from the Royal Navy, he signed on both as the captain of the *Prince of Wales* and as the commander of the two-vessel venture.

Later he said that he had been introduced to Richard by "one of the most eminent merchants of the City of London". The name of this man is unknown, but it shows that by this time, Richard had become an influential and well-connected figure in the city.

Charles Duncan was also an experienced mariner. Details of his early life are sketchy, but in 1779 he received his first warrant as "acting master" on HMS *Conqueror*. A permanent appointment followed in 1781, and Duncan served aboard several vessels during the American Revolutionary War. One of his commanders was James Burney, who had sailed with Cook on his second and third expeditions. Although this connection may well have been helpful in Duncan's appointment, he possessed more than adequate nautical, navigation, and surveying skills to have secured his post on his own merit.

Richard had appointed his youngest brother John as the supercargo on board the *Prince of Wales*. A supercargo is a representative of the ship's owner on board a merchant ship who is responsible for overseeing the cargo and its sale. John Etches possessed the same spirit of adventure as Richard and had left home with "a desire to go to sea".

Among the crew were two people who would return to the Northwest Coast as part of George Vancouver's 1791 voyage. They were Archibald Menzies, who would be the first botanist to visit the region, and James Johnstone, who was their pilot and who would become one of George Vancouver's most valuable surveyors. Vancouver would later play an important role in the future of Nootka Sound.

Menzies, a thirty-year-old Scot, was also a surgeon and had been given this role on board the *Prince of Wales*. He was a close friend of Banks. In August 1786 he had written to Banks asking him to intercede with Richard about relaxing some restrictions on private trade which were bothering him as a naturalist and historian: "It is not allowed for the ship's company to trade or barter for any curiosities. I hope, however we are not debarred from picking them up when they come our way." Banks talked to Richard, who, not wishing to upset his patron, immediately lifted the restrictions in respect of Menzies. On 29 September 1786, he wrote to Banks of how he held the young man's conduct and manners in high esteem, adding, "My younger brother is going on this voyage, and I have given him orders to pay every attention to Mr. Menzies."

Partly on Colnett's advice, Richard had forsaken his original plan, which was for the expedition to sail with only one vessel, a nearly new cutter of between 250 and 300 tons. Colnett, though, suggested that he should add "a small Sloop as a tender to the Ship, for the benefit of Trafficking and Navigating the large rivers" of the Northwest Coast.

There is no doubt that Richard's budget was adversely affected by this decision, because the principal vessel, the *Prince of Wales*, ended up as a chartered "River built ship", which was older and perhaps smaller than originally desired. It had been launched in 1752, but it was freshly fitted out for the forthcoming voyage. The tender, *Princess Royal*, was about a third of the size of her sister ship. Later Colnett described her later as "a very bad sailor".

The two ships finally left Deptford dock on 23 September 1786. Colnett's instructions for the voyage have not survived, but they probably did not differ too much from those given to Portlock and Dixon. Colnett was clearly required to build on the foundations described in Richard's first venture and to establish two trading stations, one at Nootka and another farther north.

However, there was a suggestion that financial restraints had slightly impaired the integrity of this venture when Richard issued instructions that a sealing party of fifteen men was to be taken on board and landed at Staten Island (now Isla de los Estados), off Tierra del Fuego. His intention was to set up a small sealery, that is a factory and staging post to deal with seal furs. Seal and whale hunting had begun in the area, and Richard thought that the business would develop. Staten Island was already a stopping-off point for vessels to refresh and replenish their water stocks as they rounded Cape Horn.

Richard had also mentioned "a handsome offer" he had received from a gentleman who wanted to book a passage to Tahiti, but nothing came of it. In addition, it was discovered that some unforeseen repairs had to be dealt with before the ships could depart. This led Andrew Bracey Taylor, who was the third mate on *Prince of Wales*, to comment that the repairs had "in some measure [shaken] their [the owners'] Credit in Town".

The ships sailed down the Atlantic. On 23 January 1787, after a brief stop at Cape Verde, they arrived at New Year's Harbour (now Puerto Año Nuevo) on Staten Island where a site for the sealing factory was selected and construction began. Upon the completion of this site, the fifteen-man sealing party left ship.

Knowing that the Staten Island settlement would need reinforcement, Richard had acquired a whaling ship of five hundred tons named *Duke of York* which had been built in 1780 at Archangel. She sailed on 21 April 1787, but on 11 September, shortly after her arrival at New Year's Harbour, the ship was lost. I have not been able to find the reasons for the sinking, but the area is notorious for the violence of its storms. Although the crew was saved, the disaster put an end to the factory, and the island was subsequently vacated.

After a stay of three weeks on the island, Colnett and Duncan continued their long, tedious journey northward through the Pacific, where poor weather both hindered their progress and damaged the vessels. The ships ended up spending spent five months at sea, and although there were outbreaks of scurvy, not one man died from its effects during the passage. Because of the delay, Colnett decided to head straight to Nootka Sound rather than to stop off at the Sandwich (Hawaiian) Islands as originally planned.

Reaching Friendly Cove in Nootka Sound on 4 July 1787, they found the *Imperial Eagle*, a British ship from Ostend commanded by Charles Barkley, who had no licence and was flying Austrian colours. He had been at Friendly Cove for twenty-three days and had managed to acquire all the available sea otter pelts for that season which caused Colnett a great deal of anger. Barkley soon departed, but Colnett and Duncan remained for a few weeks to carry out repairs to the ships and to allow the crews to recuperate from indications of scurvy. Menzies was also able to collect botanical specimens.

As the two ships left the Sound the following month, they met George Dixon in the *Queen Charlotte*. Discovering that they all worked for the same company, they quickly shared information. Dixon had come from Prince William Sound in the north and had advised them to check out the

Queen Charlotte Islands as it was possible that nobody had visited them yet. They made for the southern end of the islands and put into an inlet. From there they sailed north, crossing the Hecate Strait, until they reached the north-western end of a large island which Colnett named Banks Island after Sir Joseph.

Although the primary focus of the voyage was the purchase of sea otter pelts, Colnett spent a lot of time exploring the coastline in detail, apparently in a quest to locate the North-West Passage.

Having spent the winter of 1787–1788 in the Sandwich Islands, Colnett and Duncan returned to the Northwest Coast to obtain more furs. Upon arrival, the two vessels, having decided to trade separately, parted company with Colnett and the *Prince of Wales* sailing north, and with Charles Duncan and the *Princess Royal* sailing south.

After trading through the summer, the two captains reunited in the Sandwich Islands, from which point they sailed together to Canton (China) to sell their cargo of sea otter pelts, arriving around early December 1788. The furs were sold at a good profit, making their voyage "one of the more successful of the period".

The *Prince of Wales* was taken back to England via the Cape of Good Hope, but Colnett stayed on in Canton. The *Princess Royal* also remained in preparation for another two-vessel expedition, but with Thomas Hudson now as captain, replacing Charles Duncan, who wanted to return to Europe.

Having mulled over the idea of settling the Northwest Coast with convict colonies, Richard now submitted his proposals to Banks, who he knew was supportive of the one in Botany Bay, New Holland (Australia). In 1779, Banks had made a presentation to Parliament about the concept and it had been favourably received. Richard hoped that Banks would bring his plans to the attention of the government. At a meeting with him, Richard proposed that the settlement should be on the same lines as New Holland. He strongly believed that the British government should extend the New South Wales programme to the Pacific Northwest, sending out perhaps a hundred convicts with a few soldiers to keep an eye on them.

Under Richard's plan, the convict settlers would have their way paid, and all regulations laid down for the colonisation of New Holland would apply to North America. In his letter to Banks dated 17 July 1788, he also made sure that his proposal allowed opportunities for business interests, such as his own, by adding carefully, "and giving us such power over the Commercial part for a limited time as they [the government] should approve". The Hudson's Bay Company held a trade monopoly in Canada, but perhaps Richard was unaware of it. Or perhaps he was chancing his arm!

Richard urged Banks to support his concept, claiming that his plan "would not only secure the complete discovery of that extensive and unexplored part of the world, but would open and secure a source of commerce of the most extensive magnitude to this Country". Banks's interest was seized, but in raising the topic with government officials, he was persuaded that, because of the vast expense involved, convict colonies engaged in the fur trade could not be successfully established. Richard doggedly stuck to his guns, arguing that expenses would not be too large, and in any case, a given number of convicts could be transported for as little an expense as any other means of dealing with them.

Moreover, he argued that the type of establishments as he envisaged on the Northwest Coast of the Pacific would be impossible without the protection and support of the government. Once the establishments were permanently set up, they would secure the commerce of the area and the convicts' labours would be of service to the national objectives of Britain.

Richard sketched out his plan for Banks, suggesting that one or two small "factories" be set up and a small vessel be posted to the coast with a lieutenant in command who would have sufficient powers to keep the convict settlers under control. The ship could also carry out coastal surveys. Timber and fish were abundant in the Nootka Sound area, and hogs from the Sandwich Islands could be introduced. He proposed that four large well-armed shallops (light sailing boats mainly used for coastal fishing or as tenders) be employed to cruise up and down the coast and into all the inlets in search of trade. He also thought that the "Japan Islands" might be a possible market for the furs obtained by the prisoners.

In a letter to Banks dated 28 July 1788, Richard elaborated on his plan and considered the possibility of his own company planting the settlement under a government contract with the protection of "an arm'd cruiser".

According to David Mackay in his book *In the wake of Cook* Richard spoke to the crew of the *Imperial Eagle*, which had just returned from

Macao, and although this led to him abandoning the idea of a convict settlement, the information he gathered strengthened his resolve to establish a trading factory. On 30 July, he again outlined his scheme to Banks. The *Imperial Eagle* had found a strait to the south of Nootka which tended north-eastward to the interior of the continent. This proved the validity of the accounts by the Spaniards de Fuca and de Fonte and indicated that the coast was "nothing but Islands". Richard had decided to pursue another, more subtle tack. In the same area, Barkley had collected a profusion of furs. Richard again stressed the utility of forming small factories along the coast and stated his willingness "to rely on your kind assistance in the adopting of any measure that can be conducive to permanent securing of the Commerce".

A week later, Richard sought Banks's advice on one of his favourite topics: trade with Japan. In his letter of 20 July 1788, he had pointed out that Portlock and Dixon had been unable to try the Japanese market owing to "the season being too far advanced". However, his brother John had indicated that if he happened to return from the Northwest Coast to find that the trading season at Canton had ended, then he intended to take his furs to Japan. Richard questioned Banks on the chances of "opening up" that market as he was about to write to his brother by the next ship to Canton. All the merchants in the maritime fur trade declared an interest in opening a trade with Japan, but none achieved it. Portlock and Dixon never mentioned the possibility in their journals, nor did Colnett in his voyage in the *Prince of Wales*. After his release by the Spaniards in 1790, Colnett did attempt to trade with the Japanese when he found the Canton market closed. He had no success. While the opening of the market remained a possibility, the merchants used it for propaganda purposes. This was especially true in negotiations with Spain over the Nootka Crisis, when both Richard and Meares rather disingenuously claimed that the opening of the Japanese market had been imminent at the time of the seizure of their ships.

The Return of John Meares

But what about John Meares? Undaunted by the disaster he had suffered in the winter of 1786–1787, and contemptuous of Portlock's and

Dixon's attempts to gain exclusive rights to trade along the Northwest Coast, he had continued to nurture his ambition of establishing his own fur trading network that would make him a great profit as well as give him territorial claims and bring glory for Britain.

Arriving in Macao in October 1787, he had managed, within three months, to form a new trading partnership called the Merchant Proprietors with associates who had interests in India as well as in Canton. Only three of them, Daniel Beale of Beale & Co., John Henry Cox, and João Carvalho, a Portuguese merchant, were resident in China. The rest were based in India and may have included some of his former Bengal Fur Society members.

Meares had fitted out two ships:

- the 230-ton *Felice Adventurer*, commanded by Francisco José Viana but with John Meares as supercargo
- the 200-ton *Iphigenia Nubiana*, commanded by William Douglas

Meares and his associates wanted to gain exclusive control of the sea otter market at Canton and Macao by destroying the competition, namely Portlock, Dixon, and the King George's Sound Company. His plan was to arrive at Nootka Sound early enough to stake his claim to trade there. He would make this his headquarters, from which he would form an alliance with the local chief Maquinna and acquire a title to own land there. Once established at Nootka, Meares intended to explore opportunities for trade farther south at Clayoquot Sound and Barkley Sound (named after Charles Barkley, captain of the *Imperial Eagle*), travelling as far down as to the shores of Jean de Fuca Strait.

William Douglas had been instructed to sail directly to Cook Inlet in the north to begin trading and then to journey along the coastal arc south, down to the coasts of Prince William Sound and finally to Nootka Sound. He was to stop along the way wherever he thought it expedient, but he was to make sure that he would rendezvous with Meares on 1 September either in the Sound or in the Sandwich Islands.

To avoid paying the exorbitant port costs imposed by the Chinese on all foreign vessels, the ships and crew were provided with papers and passports and other papers written in Portuguese as Portugal was exempt.

The documents were intended to show that the vessels were owned by João Carvalho. The ships were mainly crewed by Portuguese sailors, although there were some Chinese carpenters on board who, once they had arrived at Nootka, would construct a forty-ton vessel from a frame that had been brought with them. They would also build a small house.

The two vessels sailed from Macao on 22 January 1788, but the need to stop off at Mindano, in the Philippines, for repairs and for heavy weather which culminated in a typhoon meant that Meares finally reached Friendly Cove in Nootka Sound on 13 May. Meares and his crew received a friendly welcome from Chief Maquinna and Chief Callicum, and he gifted them with iron, copper, and "other gratifying articles".

Meares later claimed that on 25 May, Maquinna had granted him a plot of land as a site for his headquarters. This was hotly disputed. Four years later, Maquinna, in an affidavit to the Spanish, denied that he had sold any land to Meares. This issue would have serious ramifications as we shall see in a later chapter. The house was completed on 28 May.

Next, Meares set about organising the construction of a forty-ton vessel from the frame he had brought with him from China. He also traded for sea otter furs. By 5 June, he had stored 140 skins aboard *Felice Adventurer*. There was no news of Douglas and *Iphigenia Nubiana*. Meares now decided to sail south as planned, not just to trade but also to see whether a North-West Passage really existed.

On 28 June, *Felice Adventurer* arrived at the entrance of a great inlet. This was the Strait of Juan de Fuca, a vast waterway which had already been looked at but not entered by Charles Barkley in the *Imperial Eagle* in 1787. Meares wanted desperately to explore the strait but was discouraged by the approach in canoes of hostile natives who were armed with spears and bows and arrows. Continuing south, Meares came across other sounds but was irritated at being unable to locate any anchorage points in the shallow waters. He managed to sail as far south to the mouth of the Columbia River, but he failed to appreciate its significance because of strong gales and the hazards of entering. He may have regarded it simply as a landlocked bay. His frustration is revealed in the names he gave to the river's mouth, Deception Bay, and the northern headland, Cape Disappointment, which remains to this day.

Meares's decision not to enter the Columbia River had disastrous consequences. Years later, George Vancouver, about whom more will be discussed later, sailed past the entrance in fair weather but, taking Meares's word that no river existed, continued his journey without exploring it. It was not until 11 May 1792 that the American Robert Gray from Boston, in *Columbia Rediviva*, sailed into the mouth of the river. His discovery led to the basis of the US claims to the great Pacific Northwest region. If only Meares had entered and explored the river in 1788, he would now be feted as a maritime hero and his discovery would have given Britain stronger grounds to claim all the Northwest Coast from Alaska down to San Francisco Bay.

Meares continued his exploration until 7 July, when he decided that worsening weather conditions could slow his return to Nootka Sound. On the way back, though, the weather was fine and sunny, so he decided to take advantage of it by sending a longboat into the Strait of Jean de Fuca under the command of his first officer, Robert Duffin, on a "voyage of discovery". Unfortunately, the hostility of the local natives prevented any exploration. Meares sailed to Nootka as quickly as possible.

Arriving on 26 July 1788, Meares was delighted to see that work on his little schooner was nearing completion. This would be the first nonindigenous ship to be built on the Northwest Coast. He expected his men to make a good job of it. On 8 August, Meares sailed for a brief trading visit to Clayoquot Sound. As he left the Sound, he met up with Charles Duncan in the *Princess Royal*. Duncan had had a tortuous journey around Cape Horn with only a fifteen-man crew and limited supplies. Meares provided Duncan with some emergency supplies before continuing his voyage. Meares returned, having amassed a large quantity of furs, on 24 August.

Two days later, Douglas in the *Iphigenia Nubiana* arrived from the north. He had journeyed to the Aleutian Islands and then to Cook Inlet as planned, arriving on 17 June. On 29 June, the ship left and headed north-east to Prince William Sound. He sighted Montague Island and worked his way up the channel to anchor in Snug Corner Cove at Cape Hinchinbrook. On 10 July, members of the Chenoway tribe informed him that another European ship had left the Sound a few days earlier with an enormous quantity of skins. This was later confirmed when an onshore party, sent by Douglas to gather wood, saw the following inscription on several trees:

J. Etches, *Prince of Wales*, May 9, 1788

I wonder if John Etches, the supercargo on board the *Prince of Wales*, had done this deliberately as a kind of two-fingers gesture to the rival traders who he knew would follow him!

From here, Douglas had journeyed south among the offshore islands, trading everywhere he went. In all, the skins he had amassed numbered 1,788, which, added to the 400 that Meares had obtained, constituted a highly valuable cargo for him to transport to Macao. Meares planned to depart in the *Felice Adventurer* as soon as his schooner had been launched, but Douglas and the *Iphigenia* would remain behind until the new ship was ready for sea, after which the two vessels would "prosecute the general objects" of commerce. They would then head off to the Sandwich Islands for the winter, before heading home to Macao the following spring.

The Arrival of the Americans

On 16 September 1788, a ship was sighted on the horizon. Meares's initial reaction was that the *Princess Royal* was returning in distress, but when the longboat he had sent out neared it, it was found to be the *Lady Washington*, an American sloop, under the command of Robert Gray. Gray had set sail from Boston eleven months earlier, accompanied by another ship, *Columbia Rediviva*, which was under the command of John Kendrick.

Both vessels took a route down to Cape Horn, where they had been separated by a hurricane. Gray had continued his journey northward up to their planned rendezvous, Nootka Sound, uncertain whether Kendrick and his vessel had survived. The two ships had come from Boston to trade on the Northwest Coast.

Gray had been treated to a friendly reception by Meares and his chief mate, Robert Duffin, and he invited them to dine with him aboard the *Lady Washington*. But faced with the possibility of losing sway with the natives at Nootka Sound, Meares soon set about discouraging the

American. He told Gray that trading was so poor that his vessels had not collected more than fifty skins between them. He also issued a warning about the navigational dangers that could be faced on the coast and the behaviour of the natives, describing them as having a "Monsterous Savage disposition" and cannibalistic tendencies.

Gray, though, was too wily to be taken in, saying afterwards that, despite Meares's having sworn on his "sacred word and honour" that what he had said was accurate, the "depth of his desires could easily be fathomed". He was also sceptical about the small number of skins Meares had referred to, describing his claim as a "notorious falsity".

The new schooner was launched on 19 September. Being the first nonindigenous vessel ever to be built on the Northwest Coast, she was named the *North West America*. She would be commanded by Robert Funter, one of Meares's officers and at one time William Douglas's first mate.

Launch of the North West America

On 22 September, Kendrick arrived in the *Columbia Rediviva* and Gray guided him into Nootka Sound. No doubt Gray told him about his meetings with Meares. Kendrick felt that neither of them would be able to indulge in any meaningful trade "till these Englishmen have left the place". They both felt they should spend the winter at Nootka. To speed up Meares's departure, Kendrick made his carpenters, caulkers, and blacksmiths available to assist with repairs to Meares's ships. This allowed Meares to depart in the *Felice Adventurer* on 24 September.

He had promised Maquinna that he would return in the spring of 1789 to trade and to build more houses. He considered himself very well placed and claimed that, in an elaborate ceremony, Maquinna had accepted that the Englishman was a superior being who held sovereign power over him.

Laden with his season's haul of 750 skins, Meares called in first at the Sandwich Islands. On the evening of 5 December, he eventually anchored at Macao, looking forward to a prosperous trade. But he was to receive devastating news: João Carvalho had gone bankrupt, and the Portuguese governor of Macao, with whom Carvalho had a special relationship, had died.

Meares would now have to attract new partners. His luck was in, though, because within a few days, the *Prince of Wales* and the *Princess Royal* arrived from their own season's trading on the Northwest Coast.

Associated Merchants of London and India Trading to the Northwest Coast

Meares had a very fruitful meeting with supercargo John Etches, which resulted in the former rivals becoming partners. The new venture was described as "at once a marriage of convenience and a realization by the rivals that each could profit by the other's advantageous arrangements on either side of the Pacific".

Meares would have been delighted to learn, if he had not already known, that as Richard's King George's Sound Company was able to operate under licences granted to it by the East India Company and the South Sea Company, which were valid until 1790, his ships would have no need to fly Portuguese flags.

Four ships could now be immediately readied for trade the following season: *Princess Royal*, *Iphigenia Nubiana*, *North West America*, and the *Argonaut*, which would replace the *Felice Adventurer*, which had been sold.

The principal aim of the new company would be to start a colony at Nootka with the speedy construction of a permanent factory at Friendly Cove and to engage in large-scale trade with the local natives, which had been Richard's ambition from the beginning. Colnett's sailing orders dated 3 April 1789 read:

> We look to a solid establishment, and not one that is to be abandon'd at pleasure; we authorize you to fix it at a most Convenient Station only to place your colony in Peace and Security and fully protected from the fear of the smaller Sinister Accidents.

James Colnett, who had been preparing to complete his journey by sailing home in the *Prince of Wales*, was persuaded by John Etches take command of the new venture. He was appointed overall commodore, set to journey to Friendly Cove in the *Argonaut*. Although he would be in control of all the new company ships in the Pacific, once he arrived on the Northwest Coast, his responsibility would be to implement the orders of John Meares. John Etches returned to England in the *Prince of Wales* to oversee arrangements that needed to be handled from there.

Meares was made the managing director. His role was "to remain at China, for conducting the commerce and preparing the equipment in that quarter for the US coast, and also for expediting a promising intercourse with the Japanese islands, and for completing a treaty entered into with Tyana, a prince of the Sandwich islands ... and for granting admission to all British ships to those islands".

This ambitious statement of intent drawn up by either John or Richard Etches was not entirely accurate, especially in respect to Tyana. In fact, I believe no treaty was ever discussed.

A formal agreement, which was dated 23 January 1789, created a new company which owned the joint stock of all vessels and property employed in the trade. It was to be known as the Associated Merchants of London and India Trading to the Northwest Coast of America.

The new partnership was made up of the following men:

Richard Cadman Etches, merchant of London
John Etches, merchant of London, Richard's brother
William Etches, merchant of Northampton, Richard's brother
John Meares
John Henry Cox, commander
William Fitzhugh
Henry Lane
Daniel Beale, Scottish merchant and Prussian consulate at Canton

Richard must have been extremely happy with these new arrangements as he was a great admirer of James Colnett. The falling-out with Nathaniel Portlock and George Dixon in 1788 still rankled with him as this extract from a letter he wrote to Joseph Banks on 19 May 1792 shows. He begins by praising Banks as a "warm promoter" of the first expedition in 1785, but now he had realised the following:

> [W]ith what liberality the first expedition was equipped, the encouragement to the commanders was much greater than held out to any other service, yet instead of securing their gratitude, exertions or even perseverance their conduct from leaving the Channel of England was a continual series of misconduct, disobedience of their instructions, pusillanimity, shameful waste of the property committed to their care. Had I been so fortunate to have employed a commander of Capt. Colnett's abilities, enterprise, and integrity my instructions would have been faithfully executed.

Richard was particularly upset that Portlock had neither built a trading post at Nootka Sound nor approached the potential markets in Japan, Korea, and China. Now, though, Richard was the leading partner in a venture that was committed to achieving these aims.

Argonaut and *Princess Royal* were then prepared for sail to Nootka Sound. Former captain Charles Duncan had now been replaced by Thomas Hudson. The ships were provided with plentiful stores and equipment intended to last them three years. Tied securely to the deck of the *Argonaut* was the keel and frame of a ninety-three-foot vessel which was to be completed at Nootka Sound and named the *Jason*.

James Colnett took along a contingent of Chinese artisans made up of bricklayers, carpenters, blacksmiths, tailors, seamen, and a cook. Their function was to build the "solid establishment" which was to be named Fort Pitt after the prime minister William Pitt; to build the *Jason*; and to trade with the natives. Fort Pitt would be the first of several constructions. The plan was to develop a port which would attract the local natives; allow small trading vessels to be repaired or laid up for the winter, which Robert Duffin, now first mate of the *Argonaut*, would oversee; and be a focus for other trading activities. There were also plans to bring Hawaiian men and women to settle there.

There must have been great optimism in the air at this time. The new company had the vessels, a skilled workforce, prospective settlers, knowledge of the area and weather conditions, and a friendly relationship with the local natives. What could prevent the development of an efficient, profitable network of trading ships and the beginnings of an increasingly powerful British presence on the Northwest Coast of the United States?

James Colnett sailed from Macao on 26 April 1789 and would arrive at Nootka Sound in July. Meanwhile, two days previously, the *Iphigenia Nubiana* arrived there, and a few days later, so did the *North West America*. Neither Douglas nor Funter was aware of the changed circumstances; both vessels continued to fly Portuguese flags. This confusion was to have a dramatic consequence when the *Argonaut* and *Princess Royal* arrived from China flying the British flag.

Already anchored in Nootka Sound were the *Lady Washington* and the *Columbia Rediviva*, both of which had spent the winter there. Spring had now arrived, and there was a feeling of hope and excitement in the port as the sailors busied themselves with rigging and sails in readiness for another season of trade.

The *North West America* was soon repaired, restocked, and given extra men, and Robert Funter was able to set sail again on 28 April for a trading expedition in the north. Two days later the *Lady Washington* departed with Robert Gray as captain.

Now only Douglas's *Iphigenia Nubiana* and Kendrick's *Columbia Rediviva* remained in port, when on 5 May, to their astonishment, a twenty-six-gun Spanish warship named *Princesa* sailed into the Sound under the command of Estéban José Martínez.

He had arrived on a mission: to rid the area of any foreign ships who had dared to ignore Spain's rightful claims to the North Pacific by encroaching on territory which was rightfully theirs. So keen was he to uphold Spanish claims that he had pledged to forfeit his life if he should fail his country on his mission.

Esteban José Martínez

For James Colnett, life was to take a severe downturn as, when he eventually returned to Nootka Sound, he found himself embroiled in what became known as the Nootka Crisis when he, his men, and his vessel were seized by the Spanish.

Richard would not learn of the events that followed until the early months of 1790, and when he did, it would destroy his dream of building a sea otter trading empire on the coast of the Pacific Northwest.

CHAPTER 5

THE NOOTKA SOUND INCIDENT

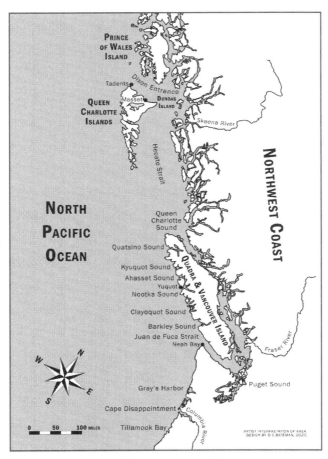

North West Coast Map

For centuries, Spain had claimed sovereignty over the whole of the West Coast of the United States. As J. Richard Nokes states in his book *Almost a Hero*:

> Spain's pretension to the Eastern Pacific as a private domain dated to the expeditions of Christopher Columbus, to Balboa's first sighting of the "Southern Sea" in 1513, to Magellan's discovery of a strait that connected the Atlantic and the Pacific in 1520, and to the discoveries of other Spanish navigators and explorers over the course of many years. In addition, three Papal Bulls in 1493 had divided the "New World" between Spain and Portugal, and the Treaty of Tordesillas in 1494 provided for a division between Spain and Portugal of all lands as yet unclaimed by other nations. Other international agreements, such as with the British in the Treaty of Madrid (1670) and the Treaty of Paris (1763), prohibited foreign vessels from entering and trading in Spanish waters in the New World. These factors, Spain believed, entitled her to an exclusive possession of territory and commerce from Cape Horn to Alaska.

But for many years, Spain, whose base was in Alta, California, had made no attempts to venture northward because there was no cause to fear foreign intrusion. In fact, the Spanish did not even have any outpost north of California. However, during the middle to later part of the eighteenth century, the situation began to change as Russian fur traders extended their activities from Siberia across into Alaska.

In retaliation, Spain began to strengthen the foothold it had already achieved in Alta, by mounting a series of explorations and reconnaissance voyages from San Blas, Mexico, to Alaska. The purpose of these voyages was not only to determine the extent of the Russian incursion but also to reinforce the claim of sovereignty the Spanish had established by right of "first discovery" and through the use of formal possession-taking rituals, which were still regarded as a meaningful part of international law.

Spain's other purpose was to search for the possible existence of the North-West Passage, the supposed sea route from the Pacific to the Atlantic Ocean. If such a route did exist and were to be discovered by another nation, such as Britain, who had already shown great interest in such a quest, the effect would be disastrous to Spain's interests on the northern Pacific coast.

The first Spaniard to sail to the far north was Juan Pérez, who, in 1774, had reached as far as the Queen Charlotte Islands. Follow-up expeditions had been launched in 1775, 1779, and 1788, from which significant information about Russian activities was acquired. This included ominous indications that Russia might be planning to seize control of Nootka Sound, which by now had become the focal point of Spain's many concerns.

Despite its not being the region's optimum port, Nootka Sound was well known and well charted, easily accessible, and usefully located as a general base of operations as well as a point of rendezvous. Over the years it had become the fur traders' primary harbour and gathering point. These factors resulted in the decision by Britain, Russia, and Spain to build a fort there so that their claims and interests could be better founded.

This startling news, coupled with the rapid increase in fur trading along the Pacific Northwest coast, mostly by British traders, although some Americans were now showing an interest, made it imperative that Spain take decisive action to uphold its firm claim of sovereignty north to 61° latitude (the vicinity of Prince William Sound, Alaska). As the first step, Spain would take occupation of Nootka Sound and thereby begin to create a new Spanish province, strategically placed north of California and south of Alaska. The strategy would also require the restriction of free trade by other nations, a policy that the Spanish had long maintained within the other lands of their empire. The British government's position, dating back to the Elizabethan period, was that British subjects had the right to navigate the oceans and to visit, trade, and create settlements in any place not already occupied by a civilised nation.

Richard's new company had therefore established its base at Nootka Sound and had entered into trading agreements with the local chieftains. A tract of land was purchased from one of them, on which the company began to create a small settlement and build warehouses.

In 1788, Estéban José Martínez was given command of an expedition to Alaska. His orders were drawn up by the viceroy of Spain, Manuel Antonio Flores, who had heard rumours of British and Russian fur trading activities and wanted to make sure that these intruders did not obtain a foothold in Nootka Sound. By sending warships to the area, Spain fully intended to protect its claim to the Northwest Coast.

Martínez was to sail from San Blas, Mexico, in the frigate *Princesa*, accompanied by the packet *San Carlos*, which was under the command of Gonzalo López de Haro. Martínez was to become a very controversial character in the Nootka Sound story. Born in Seville in 1742, he had begun his naval career at the age of thirteen. By 1773, he was serving as a second pilot at the Naval Department at San Blas. The following year, he sailed to Nootka with Pérez but was found wanting in both navigation and seamanship. For the next twelve years he held the routine job of sailing supply ships between San Blas and Monterey, and it was here, in September 1786, where he learned from a French explorer, La Pérouse, about the Russian activities in building forts, their military strength, and their plans for the future. He also learned that several British ships had arrived to exploit the sea otter trade. At heart, Martínez was a patriot. Now, impatient for an important assignment, he had been able to brief Flores about the dangers.

Martínez maintained that he been given authority by his king not only to seize any vessel that he might catch trading along the coast but also to treat all foreign sailors in the Pacific Ocean as enemies. His instructions were as precise and as exact as it was possible to make them:

> He must endeavour to obtain the goodwill of the native Indians and should he find any Russian or English ships at Nootka, he was to receive them with politeness which the existing peace demands.
>
> He was also to demonstrate to them with just reason why Spain had claimed this part of the coast as her very own and the methods his superior government were adopting to carry out these claims.
>
> All this he must explain with prudent firmness but without being led into harsh expressions, which may give offence and cause rupture. Should the foreigners attempt to use force he was to repel it the extent that they are employed.

His subsequent actions in Nootka Sound showed that he had badly misread his instructions.

Martínez Arrives in Nootka Sound

Upon his arrival in Nootka Sound on the foggy morning of 5 May, Martínez made some startling discoveries. Not only did he see the *Iphigenia Nubiana* and the *Columbia Rediviva* in the harbour, but also, having dropped anchor opposite the village of Yuquot, he went ashore to discover a whole colony of people comprised mainly of Chinese labourers, together with a few men and women from the Sandwich Islands.

Initially, Martinez's dealings with the captains and the officers of the two ships, one British and one American, went well. He invited Douglas, Kendrick, and their officers to dine with him aboard the *Princesa*, and a few days later, the Spanish were in turn invited to dine aboard the *Columbia Rediviva* and *Iphigenia Nubiana*.

Although Martínez may have been slightly suspicious of the Americans, he did not see them as a threat—at least not at first. He was also tolerant of Douglas and the *Iphigenia Nubiana*, which was anchored several miles away, even spending several days aboard her. Douglas was unwell at the time, though, and was looking forward to seeing the arrival of Meares in the *Felice Adventurer*.

But when, on 12 May, another Spanish warship, the *San Carlos*, captained by Gonzalo López de Haro, arrived in the bay, Martínez's attitude completely changed. Perhaps he had been using his soft approach only until the arrival of his colleague. Now, the addition of extra firepower would make him feel more secure and give him more resolve.

Two mornings later, he demanded to see Douglas's papers, but as they were written in Portuguese, neither man could understand them. Martínez called upon his interpreters, who were Spanish padres, to translate them, but the assumptions they made were hotly disputed by Douglas. The charge against him and his crew was that, without licence and carrying illegal instructions, they had illegally entered Spanish territory and violated their sovereignty. Douglas had his own Portuguese-speaking man within the crew, but he seemed unwilling to intervene. Douglas began to suspect that Kendrick was in some way complicit in Martínez's actions against him.

Douglas was then arrested. Around fifty Spanish officers and other men boarded *Iphigenia Nubiana* and hoisted Spanish colours. They also seized the ship's supplies, the cannons, trade goods, equipment, the captain's log, papers, charts—almost every moveable object. The British crew was taken aboard the two Spanish warships and held there.

Secretly, Douglas managed to get word to the Indian chief Maquinna, asking that if he were to see the *Felice Adventurer* and *North West America* approaching the Sound, would he forewarn them of the dangers they faced. Sensing the tension and possible danger, Maquinna moved his village some miles farther away to avoid being drawn into the dispute.

Martínez now set about transforming Nootka Sound into a possession of the Spanish Empire. At its entrance he created "Fort San Miguel", which he hoped would ward off any Russian or English expeditions. At strategic points by the harbour, he erected cannon emplacements. And he began building a military settlement to accommodate about two hundred occupants.

Martínez's strategy for his prisoners was to send Douglas and half his British crew, held in irons, to the Spanish headquarters in San Blas, Mexico. The other half would be transferred back to the *Iphigenia Nubiana*, which would now be under the command of Martínez's Spanish officers. The reason for this was that although the ship had been careened and made ready for sail, Martínez realised that he would not have enough of his own people to man her. But he was annoyed to discover that the crew remained steadfastly loyal to Douglas and that they would refuse to serve under Spanish colours.

Through his own headstrong actions, Martínez had put himself into an embarrassing position—and he needed to find a way of resolving it. So, on 22 May, the day that the ship was due to sail to San Blas, one of his interpreters was asked to take another look at Douglas's papers. This time he concluded that "the papers very good", and all charges against Douglas were dropped. Several days later, the British seamen and the *Iphigenia Nubiana*, fresh from its refit at the Spaniards' expense, were released. Two days later, Martínez asked Douglas to sign a paper stating that the British had been well-treated. At first Douglas refused to sign, but later, to break the deadlock, he changed his mind.

Martínez was almost certainly aware that the *Iphigenia Nubiana* was not a Portuguese ship, but he accepted the plea that Douglas's intentions had always been honourable: he had only entered the Sound because he needed to make repairs to his ship and replenish his supplies so that he could continue his journey. Douglas was permitted to gather adequate supplies and equipment to get him to the Sandwich Islands and then onwards to Macao. On the assurance that Douglas would not start trading anywhere along the coast, Martínez gave him permission to depart on 1 June.

With only sixty to seventy otter skins on board, Douglas had no intention of journeying to Macao. So, setting off northward, he managed over a period of nearly a month, during which he had several encounters with local tribesmen, to trade for 760 prime sea otter skins. He finally left the North Pacific coast for the Sandwich Islands on 28 June and eventually arrived at Macao on 5 October 1789. Here he was able to describe to Meares the hostility that he had experienced from the Spanish while in Nootka Sound.

What Douglas did not know was that other ships had sailed into the Sound and had received similar treatment from Martínez.

On 8 June 1789, just a few days after Douglas's departure, Robert Funter had re- entered Nootka Sound in the *North West America* and was met by two Spanish launches. In the harbour, instead of seeing *Iphigenia Nubiana*, Funter saw two Spanish warships. The events that followed resembled those that had happened to Douglas.

On the first evening, Martínez invited Funter and his chief officer to dine aboard one of the Spanish warships. The next day, Martínez boarded the *North West America*, searched it, and demanded to see Funter's papers before seizing the ship and arresting the British and Chinese crews on similar charges to those levied at Douglas.

The sea otter skins that the ship was carrying, numbering over two hundred, were unloaded and transferred to the hulls of the Spanish ships. Martínez had concluded that the sea otter trade could be very profitable. He also decided to sequester the *North West America* and to use her for his own trade and exploration. The ship was beached, and the Spaniards set about repairing it, including patching up the hull, which had been ravaged by shipworm.

This little ship, the first European vessel to be built on the US coast, was renamed *Santa Gertrudis la Magna* by Martínez. It never flew the Union Jack again.

At dusk on 15 June, as Captain Thomas Hudson arrived at the

entrance of Nootka Sound in the *Princess Royal*, the two Spanish launches approached him as they had done with Funter. Slightly alarmed at this, Hudson immediately ordered his crew to put their vessel into a state of defence.

Although surprised to be greeted by Spaniards, he responded in a friendly manner, pointing out his right as a mariner to enter and refit his ship after a long and arduous voyage. In the case of the *Princess Royal*, he had been at sea for 116 days. He saw that the Spaniards were accompanied by Robert Funter, who, at the earliest opportunity, told Hudson all about the actions the Spaniards had taken regarding the *Iphigenia Nubiana* and the *North West America*.

Martínez examined Hudson's papers, which were not written in Portuguese. Seeming to find them in order, he allowed the sea otter pelts that he had confiscated from the *North West America* to be transferred to the *Princess Royal*. Hudson was then given permission to leave on the understanding that his ship risked confiscation should he return to any harbour south of Prince William Sound. Before his departure, Hudson managed to write three letters, which he wanted to be passed to Captain Colnett, who, he knew, would be arriving imminently. Although two of the letters contained partially concealed warnings about the aggressive attitude of the Spaniards, they met with their approval. The third letter had been composed secretly and was to be given to Maquinna for forwarding to Colnett.

Hudson left Nootka Sound on 2 July, and despite Martínez's warning, he continued to trade for sea otter furs. At the same time, Colnett was arriving offshore in the *Argonaut*, and from some distance away through the fog, he sighted the *Princess Royal*, but there was no reason for him to attempt to contact her.

Colnett was totally unaware of the crisis that was beginning to unfold in the Sound. As a partner in the newly formed Associated Merchants enterprise set up by Meares and the Etches brothers, who held licences from the East India and South Sea companies, his ship was flying the Union Jack, as had the *Princess Royal*. The enterprise planned to build permanent headquarters in Nootka Sound, but the Spaniards had no intention of letting it do so.

Once the *Argonaut* had anchored off the entrance to the Sound, two boats came towards it out of the darkness. In one were Martínez and some Spanish troops; in the other, Captain Gray, the American, and several sailors. Martínez was not wearing his uniform. He was viewed with some suspicion as he came aboard, until he managed to establish his rank. Colnett was amazed to be greeted by Spaniards, as had been the earlier British visitors.

Some discussion was had over rival British and Spanish rights, but there was no sign of animosity, and Colnett seemed prepared to dismiss the warnings contained in the one letter from Hudson that had been passed to him, as well as the verbal warnings from the Americans. Funter had suggested that it would be prudent for Colnett to anchor outside the port until the following morning, but he decided to accept Martínez's offer to be towed into the harbour.

Later, in his journal, Colnett maintained that he had instructed his chief mate, Robert Duffin, to make sure that the *Argonaut* was anchored near to the mouth of the harbour, from where departure would be easy. Colnett went below and enjoyed a convivial time with Martínez, where they "drank freely", but he wrote that when he went up on deck, he discovered that his vessel was "in the centre of the Cove" under the sixteen guns of the Spanish boat *San Carlos*. It was also being made fast to the *Columbia Rediviva* and the Spanish flagship, *Princesa*, which had twenty-one guns. Colnett only possessed the limited firepower of two swivel guns because his twelve cannons had been stored in the hold.

A clerk from the *Columbia Rediviva* delivered Hudson's second letter to Colnett. This one, like the first, revealed that Martínez had taken possession of Meares's *North West America*. But still this did not seem to alarm him. He wrote later, "As neither of the letters I receiv'd gave one any apprehension I gave up all thought of suspicion." But much later, on hearing about Hudson's third letter, intended to be delivered by Maquinna, and containing stronger warnings, Colnett altered his stance, claiming, "It would have saved my ship had I received it."

Following breakfast aboard the *Princesa*, the captains exchanged visits. Colnett agreed to share some of his supplies with the Spaniards. Martínez identified a member of Colnett's crew, a boatswain, as a native of Spain, and Colnett agreed that he could be transferred to him. In fact, the man was from British-held Gibraltar. At this stage, the cordiality began to evaporate.

Having announced his intended departure, Colnett again boarded the *Princesa*. He was surprised to be greeted by Martínez, some Spanish officers, a Spanish padre, and some American officers. Martínez immediately demanded to see Colnett's papers. Later, Colnett claimed that he had placed his papers on the table but that Martínez had declined to read them, saying that they were forged. Martínez claimed that Colnett had shown him his passport, which was written on parchment and supposedly signed by George III, but he had declined to let Martínez read it, adding that he was not authorised to show anyone the instructions he had received.

Martínez then announced that he had orders from His Catholic Majesty to seize all British ships that he might encounter in waters claimed by Spain.

Both men were stretching the truth: all that Martínez had were orders from the viceroy of New Spain to discourage any British and Russian ships that he might encounter in the area. As we have seen earlier in this chapter, he had no directive to seize any ships unless he feared attack. All Colnett had was a lengthy set of instructions which John Meares had signed on behalf of the Associated Merchants.

A heated argument now developed in which both men lost their tempers. Colnett said that he intended to depart immediately, but Martínez refused him permission. Colnett insisted he would leave even if the Spanish forced him to strike colours (that is to lower his flag in an admission of surrender). According to Martínez, Colnett had insulted the Spanish flag and Spanish authority. There was confusion as to what happened next. Martínez stated that two or three times Colnett had placed his hand on his sword as if to threaten him in his own cabin and had called him "a God damned Spaniard".

Martínez maintained that he had acted with prudence and had tried to mollify Colnett by all possible means to make him calm down and produce the papers as requested. At the same time, it occurred to him that if Colnett were permitted to leave Nootka, he would no doubt return at some stage to take possession of it. Colnett had already told him that it was his intention to build a settlement in Nootka Sound. Alternatively if Colnett decided to head directly home to England, the British government would be able to take decisive action long before the Spaniards would be able to defend themselves. In either case, Martínez thought that, to prevent Colnett from sailing, he would have no option but to open fire on the *Argonaut*—and this would probably cost the lives of his crewmen.

So, to avoid any bloodshed, Martínez decided to arrest Colnett there and then in his cabin. According to Colnett, Martínez flew out of the cabin, and three or four sailors entered with muskets. One cocked a musket at Colnett's chest while another snatched his short sword from him. A third sailor "collared me and tore my shirt and coat". Stocks were ordered for Colnett's legs, but an American officer who had been in the British navy advised against it. Instead, Colnett was confined as a close prisoner in the cabin. Martínez declared him a prisoner of war together with all his officers, crew, and ship and told him that he would be sent to San Blas, Mexico, to be dealt with by the viceroy of New Spain.

Colnett was held in custody by the Spaniards in San Blas and was not released until May 1790. His ship the *Argonaut* was then returned to his command. On 9 July, when he was permitted to sail, he headed north to Clayoquot Sound, where he resumed his fur trading activities. Revisiting Nootka Sound in 1791, he was told that it was now Spanish territory and that he was not allowed to trade with the local natives. Undaunted, he spent five months trading along the coast and managed to obtain over a thousand furs.

During his time in captivity, Colnett had made many protests about his treatment and had sent many letters. On 1 May 1790 he had written to the British ambassador in Madrid, to his mother, and to Richard protesting about Spain's "piracy and ill treatment to the subjects of Great Britain".

A picture called *Spanish Insult to the British Flag at Nootka Sound, 1789,* after an engraving by R. Dodd, published 1791

Meares's Memorial

Working in Macao, attending to the business of the Associated Merchants, Meares was unaware of the events that had taken place in Nootka Sound until the arrival of William Douglas in the *Iphigenia Nubiana* on 5 October 1789. Douglas's information was incomplete. It was not until 17 November, when the *Columbia Rediviva*, under Robert Gray's command, arrived, that Meares was able to receive the whole picture. The crew of the *North West America* were on board, and Robert Funter gave Meares several confidential letters from Robert Duffin describing the events that had taken place following the arrival of Martínez. Meares asked Funter and some members of his crew to prepare an affidavit condemning what they perceived as "Spanish perfidy". Once he had collected all information and obtained sworn statements from both crews, Meares booked his passage to London. As the managing director of the Associated Merchants, he had a duty to protect his trading enterprise as well as British interests. He probably left Macao for London around 5 December 1789. The name of the ship he sailed in is no longer known, but he arrived in London in mid-April, having stopped off in the Philippines for a few days.

During the long voyage, he began to compose a summary of the events at Nootka. This became known as the Meares Memorial. As well as contacting the government on his arrival, Meares immediately met with John Etches and was able to provide him with more details of the seizure. Etches, in turn, passed the information onto Richard, who was then residing in Calais, France.

If Meares had been expecting to be the initial bearer of this news to London, he was in for a disappointment because London's first indication had arrived long before him. It had been sent in a 4 January 1790 dispatch from Arthur Merry, the British chargé d'affaires in Madrid, who had learned of the incident from Spanish sources. The account he provided, though, addressed to the Duke of Leeds, the foreign secretary, was lacking in detail and mistakenly stated that a Russian ship had been present. Richard first learned about the seizure of his ships in January or February.

On 25 January 1790, Spain's ambassador to the Court of St James, the Marquis de Campo, handed Leeds an official protest which contained a more accurate account of events and sought an assurance that

> His Majesty, George III, will certainly not fail to give the strictest orders to prevent such attempts in the future, and to punish such undertakings in a manner to restrain his subjects from continuing them on these lands which have been occupied by the Spaniards.

Leeds responded to the Spanish with a terse note insisting on the British right to trade and settle in the area, a right which would be "asserted and maintained with a proper degree of vigour". He went on to demand that the seized ships should be returned and compensation be paid. Until these issues had been resolved, he was not prepared to entertain any further discussions with them. The prime minister, William Pitt, had never been entirely happy with his foreign secretary, and he felt that he had taken a tough stance without knowing the full facts and therefore had exacerbated the situation unnecessarily.

On 26 February, therefore, he sent off a more conciliatory letter which requested full information and justification for the incident while still demanding that Martínez return the seized property and pay compensation.

For some weeks, the issue remained dormant on the desks of the diplomats while both Britain and Spain awaited receipt of more accurate information as to exactly what had happened on the Northwest Coast. Aware that news would probably take a year to arrive from there, the British readied a small naval expedition, while the Spanish chose to alert their ally France to the situation, as well as to begin a small-scale military preparation.

When Meares arrived in London in April 1790, he was urged by Pitt to complete his Memorial as quickly as possible. The information he provided would prove to be invaluable to Pitt in his dispute with Spain. The account confirms that several British ships had been seized and that British captives had been ill-treated in Mexican prisons. Meares also confirmed that the Spanish were trying to claim as their own territories land which he had already claimed for Britain in the name of George III.

Around this time, news came from Arthur Merry that Spain was now involved in naval preparation and that fourteen ships of the line were being fitted.

On 30 April, Meares presented his Memorial to William Wyndham Grenville, the Home Secretary, and then on 13 May it was read to both houses of Parliament. Pitt told the Commons that the Spanish claim was:

> the most absurd and exorbitant that could be imagined; a claim of which they had never heard of before, which was indefinite in its extent, and which originated in no treaty. … If that claim were given way to, it must deprive this country of the means of extending its navigation and fishery in the Southern Ocean, and would go towards excluding His Majesty's subjects from an infant trade, the future extension of which could not but prove essentially beneficial to the commercial interests of Great Britain.

Meares's Memorial was then distributed to the British public, who were completely taken by surprise at the events which were unfolding. Government stock began to fall in the markets. Pitt was so keen to take advantage of Meares's testimony that he had already used it to incite his cabinet to demand immediate satisfaction for the "outrages committed" and to request King George III to authorise a mobilisation for war.

The King went along with Pitt's wishes, and the Treasury assigned a sum of £1,000,000 for military expenditure. Preparations began for the navy to fit out forty ships of the line, and Lord Howe was brought out of retirement to take command. As his flagship, he planned to use HMS *Queen Charlotte*, a vessel of a hundred guns or more. Sailors were to be recruited for duty during "the Spanish Armament", using press gangs if necessary.

Interestingly, lots of United States sailors were press-ganged, so much so that the captains of US vessels in port appealed to the American statesman, Gouverneur Morris for aid. Morris was on a private visit but had been asked by Washington to investigate the ministry's disposition towards the US. Having spoken to Pitt and Leeds, he had been given assurances that Great Britain had no wish to molest US citizens and that the problem had arisen because of the difficulty of distinguishing between the US subjects and the subjects of His Majesty.

Britain, as well as Spain, now had a lot at stake. Britain's exploration and settlement in the Pacific had only just commenced, and although the right to trade in sea otter furs from the Northwest Coast was important, there were other considerations. For example, a lucrative whaling industry could be established in the Pacific. The first British penal colony in New Holland (Australia) had only been set up two years previously; similar colonies could be established along the Pacific Coast. In any case, a claim to an enormous mass of territory from a country that Britain had fought against in wars three times over the past fifty years was unacceptable. To Pitt, the Nootka incident presented an opportunity to undermine Spain's claim to exclusive sovereignty of the entire Pacific coast of the Americas. An apology from Spain about the capture and release of the British ships and the insult to the British flag would not suffice. He wanted to establish the freedom for ships flying the British flag to sail and trade along the sea lanes of the Pacific Ocean and, where coasts were unoccupied, to set up colonies.

On 6 May, Richard sent a lengthy letter to Banks from Calais. He told him that he had received Meares's official account of the seizure of his ships and the "whole of the establishments on the N.W. Coast" via his brother John.

Richard was fully aware that the British government had already made demands on Spain for the return of the seized ships and for compensation to be paid. His letter therefore is mainly a highly exaggerated declaration of his entitlements, his achievements on the Northwest Coast, and the potential for future profits. For example, he gives the impression that two establishments had been set up: "in K.G. Sound and another to the Northward", the latter presumably the Queen Charlotte Islands. But the only achievement in this respect was the small wooden house that John Meares had set up while at Nootka in 1788. Richard berates Portlock and Dixon, maintaining that had they obeyed their orders, they would have seen off all competition, and instead of sustaining a loss of "seven thousand pounds and upward", Richard would have made his fortune. In fact, both captains had made strong counteraccusations against Richard, with Portlock declaring that, while falling short of expectations, the first expedition had still provided a substantial yield for him, his company, and his sponsors.

The trading season for sea otter furs ran roughly from May to October. Richard makes the point that as his ships were seized "with half the season over", that is midway through it, the number of furs obtained at that stage was much lower than would have been expected for a whole season. Therefore, he felt that this should be taken into consideration in the calculation of Spain's restitution.

Richard adds that had he been allowed to build small craft at Nootka, the probability of finding the North-West Passage would have increased to a certainty. He implies that had the Spaniards not imprisoned him, Colnett no doubt would have continued exploring the Northwest Coast and may well have discovered a river or waterway which would lead to the other side of the continent.

He also claims that by the time Martínez had arrived, the "principles of a permanent and regular system of Commerce; on a wide and extensive scale" had been founded and that there was every prospect of selling furs "and American produce" to Japan, as well as "establishing a very valuable fishery".

The letter ends with Richard praising Banks as a "warm and strenuous patronizer of the first Enterprise", adding that he feels confident that Banks will use his "friendly endeavours, in our obtaining ample restitution", and he hopes that Banks will provide his support for him "in obtaining a preference in any future Enterprise".

Banks's response to Richard's letter, if indeed there was one, has not survived.

When Spain eventually replied to Pitt's letter, their response was haughty. And as war clouds gathered, they too began to mobilise. They called upon France to become their ally under the so-called Bourbon Family Compact, but France, in the early throes of revolution, was hesitant about becoming involved. Without them, Spain would be left without its key ally. Spain also asked for help from Austria, Russia, and the United States but did not receive satisfactory responses. Prussia and Holland had agreed to support England.

Pitt was gambling that Spain would not be keen now to go to war over such a small part of the globe, but many in the British government were not so convinced. Their announcements, parliamentary and public oratory, newspapers, and other publications created propaganda which soon reached fever pitch. Meares's Memorial had been released to the public, and influential people promoted the printing of florid pamphlets written by Richard and John Etches and the undersecretary of foreign affairs, Sir James Bland Burges.

Meares, meanwhile, was keen to outline the importance of the fur trade in the commerce between the United States and China. On 27 May 1790, he addressed the Privy Committee for Trade. He also continued preparing the narrative of his exploits, which were published as "Voyages". The list of subscribers who supported its publication is impressive: His Royal Highness the Prince of Wales is followed by the Duke of Leeds, the Earl of Effingham, Sir Joseph Banks, Evan Nepean, and many others, 350 names which included the three Etches brothers—Richard, William, and John.

The controversy between London and Madrid dragged on into the summer of 1790. In June, Pitt asked George III to dissolve Parliament and call a general election. Although this resulted in a small increase in Pitt's Commons majority, he found himself being criticised on the one hand for inaction in resolving the issue and on the other hand for potentially exposing Britain to an expensive and unnecessary war.

Meanwhile, Spain's preparations for a possible war continued, but they suffered a setback when the decision by Louis XVI to support Spain with French naval mobilisation was debated in the National Assembly, where it was decreed that the king should no longer have the power to enter into a war without the Assembly's permission.

In July, Pitt sent another missive to Madrid, demanding "an Admission, that the Court of Spain was not in possession of Nootka Sound" but accepting that "any further Grounds of Claim … will still be open to discussion".

Pitt's revised terms dated 14 October carried a warning that if Spain did not accept his ultimatum within ten days, Spain would face an attack.

The new king of Spain, Carlos IV, aware that he would almost certainly be without France, his major ally, and having been unable to secure the support of Russia and Austria, decided to instruct his chief negotiator, the Conde de Floridablanca, to give in to Pitt's immediate demands, although this still left a number of unresolved issues.

The threat of war remained. When, belatedly, the French National Assembly agreed to fit out forty-five ships of the line to Spain, tensions between London and Paris escalated with France being warned on no account to supply any of its fleet to Spain.

In Madrid, the detailed British proposals continued to be debated, and on 28 October 1790 at the Escorial Palace to the north of the capital, the two nations agreed the first of three treaties, known as the Nootka Conventions.

Britain rejoiced at the end of the confrontation, which had been achieved without a shot being fired, but in truth, several issues still needed to be settled.

Under the First Nootka Convention, Spain agreed to release any British ships and seamen still held captive. The tract of land that Meares said he had purchased from the natives and on which he had erected a building was to "be restored to the said British subjects". The agreement also gave Britain and Spain equal rights to navigate, trade, and whale fish "in the Pacific Ocean or in the South Seas" and to establish settlements on lands not occupied by Spain.

In Britain's view, these lands extended along the Pacific coast from San Francisco northward to the Russian claims in Alaska. To Pitt, the ancient "New Albion" of Sir Francis Drake was now wide open to discovery and settlement, but to the Spanish, it meant only the area north of Nootka.

Ironically, Martínez's actions, which he had taken to protect Spain's interests in the North Pacific, marked the beginning of the end of Spain's pretensions there.

On 26 November 1790, the late session of Parliament contained an announcement of peace. The thirty-seven British warships that had been at sea returned to port. Pitt's strategy of holding back from submitting his final ultimatum to Spain until British military preparations had been completed, and at the point when Spain could not be sure who its allies were, had resulted in a victory without a war. Pitt had now become a confident statesman on the world stage. The naval mobilisation and the stand-off with Spain had cost Britain £3,133,000, a sum much higher than the original estimate of £1,000,000, and one that Pitt planned to pay off within four years through temporary taxation.

How this decision affected Richard can only be guessed at, but he must have had financial worries. He had hoped that the East India Company, the South Sea Company, and the British government would provide preferential treatment for the troubles that he and his associates were going through. He and Meares made requests of those three entities in this respect, but nothing came of them. However, it is believed that the money received by way of indemnity and compensation from Spain was certainly fair enough, and what is now known about the circumstances of the trade at the time certainly justifies the assumption that if the Associated Merchants' trade had not been hampered by the Spaniards, their net profit would have been considerably less than the profit they received from the Spanish money.

George Vancouver

The next stage was to implement the terms of the First Nootka Convention and to secure British rights in the Pacific, which included the acceptance of the formal surrender of the land seized by Spain. To achieve this, the Admiralty appointed a young naval officer named George Vancouver. He was born in the thriving and important seaport of King's Lynn, Norfolk, on 22 June 1757.

A portrait believed to be of George Vancouver

Although only thirty-two years of age, Vancouver had served his country since the age of thirteen, when he had first joined the Royal Navy, enlisting as an able seaman. He was, however, destined to become a career sailor on track to promotion to midshipman and then to the rank of lieutenant. He was fortunate to have been chosen to sail under James Cook on his second and third voyages, visiting the South Pacific, the Sandwich Islands, and the Northwest Coast. Upon his return to Britain in October 1780, he was commissioned as a lieutenant and served on the sloop HMS *Martin*, spending the next year patrolling the North Sea and English Channel. By now, the American Revolutionary War was going badly for Britain and had spread to a full-scale European involvement. The American colonies had secured the support of both France and Spain, and Russia, Denmark, Sweden, and the Netherlands had joined up to form an Armed Neutrality. In October 1781, the British finally surrendered to the Americans at Yorktown, and while the peace terms were being negotiated, HMS *Martin* was ordered across the Atlantic to the Caribbean, where both

French and Spanish fleets had assembled. Having taken part in a terrifying sea battle with a Spanish ship, Vancouver was later promoted to junior lieutenant aboard *Fame*, where his duties became more routine, although conditions aboard the vessel were extremely poor. Vancouver returned to England in July 1783. War had now ended, and he was on half pay while he waited for another commission. He was in a fortunate position, having acquired an extensive set of skills in hydrography and navigation, and it was not long, November 1784, before his reputation and connections secured a posting as third lieutenant aboard the *Europa*, about to leave for Jamaica. During his stay in the region, Vancouver carried out marine surveys, obtaining hydrographic information about key harbours. He received high praise for his work. On 13 February 1788, he was promoted to first lieutenant. The *Europa* arrived in Plymouth in September 1789. Having been away for almost five years, Vancouver was paid off, but once again it was not long before he was in demand. Vancouver's friend and patron Sir Alan Gardner, who had been appointed one of the Lords of the Admiralty, proposed that he be sent on an interesting voyage of exploration which would suit his exact set of skills. A new vessel named *Discovery* in honour of James Cook's ship had been built and was being prepared for a voyage into the South Atlantic—either in the vicinity of South Africa or into the southern whale fishing areas.

But then the Nootka Crisis changed everything. During the Spanish armament in 1790, Vancouver had been posted as third lieutenant aboard the *Courageous* under the command of Sir Alan Gardner. The ship had been engaged in manoeuvres in the English Channel. Vancouver had been promoted to first lieutenant. Gardner had recommended him to the decision makers at the Admiralty, and in November 1790 he was summoned to a meeting. The following month he was confirmed as commander of *Discovery*.

At the height of the Nootka Crisis, Richard's brother John Etches wrote a pamphlet charging that the Spanish "have the keys of the whole Pacific, to the exclusive monopoly of an ocean and its numerous islands, which embrace in their extent almost half the globe". Vancouver's mission was intended to change all that. But in addition to reclaiming British territory and restoring British honour at Nootka Sound, he was to carry out certain scientific and geographical objectives.

During the early months of 1791, Vancouver's exact orders for the voyage were heavily debated and amended. He received his final instructions on 8 March 1791. His overall objective was to "acquire a more complete knowledge, than has yet been obtained, of the north-west coast of America", but this was broken down into more specific activities such as the nautical surveying of the coastline from Baja, California, northward to Cook Inlet, Alaska. This included gathering information on the Spanish defences to the south of California and those of the Russians to the north.

It was believed that a river might flow from the interior into Cook Inlet, which could have commercial benefits, especially to the Hudson's Bay Company. Vancouver was specially asked to search for it and to look for any evidence of a North-West Passage. He was also asked to search for the supposed Strait of Anián, where a passageway might lead into lakes in the interior referred to as the "inland sea". The winter months were to be spent in the Sandwich Islands, where Vancouver was to occupy himself "very diligently in the examination and survey of the said islands".

His orders stressed that he should be friendly towards any Spanish ships and captains that he might meet during his journey and offer to share any geographical information with them. In his dealings with the native people, he should judiciously provide them with presents and "by all other means ... conciliate their friendship and confidence".

The final objective of the expedition was to implement the Nootka Agreement and to retrieve from the Spanish the land and property claimed by John Meares. Any British subjects who might still be living under the control of the Spanish should be "relieved", especially any Chinese labourers who had been brought to Nootka by John Meares. Although this final objective was obviously the main reason for the voyage, the information handed to Vancouver was both vague and ambiguous. Over several days, British officials had questioned Meares under oath to determine the precise nature of the property he claimed was owned by him and the Etches consortium. He said that he had provided Chief Maquinna with "considerable presents" for a property which was about an acre in size and included a large house which could shelter around thirty-five people. Meares also claimed to have negotiated with another leader, Chief Wickaninnish, for the right to build a similar factory farther south at Clayoquot Sound.

Meares was being deliberately vague in his descriptions so that he would not be able to be pinned down later as an inveterate liar. He was playing a very dangerous game, hoping to cheat both the British and Spanish governments, but eventually his credentials as a lieutenant in the Royal Navy and his association with Richard, who was well connected politically, would ensure that he received some "compensation" from the Spanish government. Meares, though, was not entirely happy with the amount he received as we shall see later.

Vancouver, however, departed having been told that he would have to await further details about the "particular instructions" of the land and the structures he would be expected to retrieve from the Spanish. On 1 April 1791 he left Falmouth in the HMS *Discovery* with HMS *Chatham* serving as tender.

By way of the Cape of Good Hope, the ships sailed across to Australia and New Zealand, and from there on to Tahiti and the Sandwich Islands, during which coastline surveys were undertaken and botanical specimens collected at each stop. Then, just over a year after his departure from England, on 18 April 1792, Vancouver sighted the West Coast of the United States at 39° 27 N, near Cape Mendocino, on the California coast, near present-day San Francisco.

With minute care, he began his survey of the coast as the ships journeyed northward, entering the tricky channels and inlets in the region of what later became known as Vancouver Island, Puget Sound, and the Gulf of Georgia. The treacherous coastline would mean that most of this work could only be undertaken in small craft propelled by both sail and oar in the dangerous uncharted waters.

Vancouver was not in a great hurry to complete his surveys and rush to meet the Spanish negotiator, Bodega y Quadra, at Friendly Cove. Firstly, he regarded the cartographic survey programme as his own personal mission, and he wanted to complete as much of it as possible before the end of the short summer season. Secondly, aware of the paucity of his current instructions, he was expecting his supply ship *Daedalus* to arrive soon with additional ones, and he wanted to avoid meeting Bodega y Quadra before he had reviewed those instructions. By late August, Vancouver had reached a point midway to Alaska where he came upon a British fur trader, *Venus*, whose captain informed them that both *Daedalus* and Bodega y Quadra were waiting for his arrival at Friendly Cove, Yuquot.

Juan Francisco de la Bodega y Quadra

Juan Francisco de la Bodega y Quadra, the new commander of the Pacific squadron at San Blas who had been appointed by the king of Spain to set the boundaries for his country's empire in the north-west, had arrived at Nootka in March. He was a renowned naval explorer and a Peruvian-born aristocrat proud of his Castilian blood. A gentleman, he was educated, intelligent, and sophisticated—a man of letters and a man of action. He was a Spanish patriot who was intent on obtaining the best possible deal from the man the British had sent to meet him at Friendly Cove.

Upon his arrival, Bodega y Quadra soon got down to business, and he had a lot of repair work to do since the killing of Chief Callicum by one Martínez's men had led to most of his people being reluctant to have anything to do with the Spanish. He began by meeting and cultivating a friendly relationship with Chief Maquinna, who was invited to dine with him, as were other native leaders, who also accepted the invitation to share his table. Bodega y Quadra began to establish himself as a kind of chief, sharing his generosity, friendship, and hospitality with both the local natives and the visitors who came in their ships to Friendly Cove. They were all invited to dine each night at his great hall ashore.

He also went to work interviewing Maquinna and the merchant captains on their opinions of Martínez, Colnett, and Meares's claims over his lost property.

He concluded that Meares's version of the series of events which led to the Nootka Crisis was at least partially false and probably completely so. The captains, Robert Gray of the *Columbia Rediviva* and Joseph Ingraham of the *Lady Washington*, both of whom had witnessed Martínez's actions against Colnett, provided him with written testimony that events were closer to Martínez's version than to that of Meares. They also claimed to be unaware that Maquinna had sold any land to Meares. According to the Portuguese captain of Meares's ship *Iphigenia Nubiana*, when Martínez arrived, Meares had no significant establishment, factory, or house apart from a "very small house", "made from a few boards got from Indians", which was pulled down when the ship sailed. Maquinna denied ever selling him any land, let alone the entire harbour.

These testimonials were almost certainly biased, distorted not only by the passing of time and the vagaries of memory but also by the shifting political balance along the coast. The local natives and the fur traders possibly felt that their interests would be better served by having the European side of the fur trade controlled and managed by the amiable Bodega y Quadra and the Spanish rather than by unknown and potentially exploitative British consortiums.

The arrival of *Discovery* and *Chatham* in Friendly Cove was greeted with a ceremonious welcome by the Spanish mariners. Vancouver and Bodega y Quadra met in front of a great two-storey house in the village in which the Spaniard had arranged "a grand entertainment" for all the

British and Spanish officers. A sumptuous five-course meal was served on plates of solid silver.

The two men got on well at their initial meeting despite neither being able to speak each other's language—an embarrassing oversight by both governments—but Vancouver was fortunate to find a fluent Spanish speaker aboard the *Daedalus* who could act as his interpreter.

While both men enjoyed the pleasantries, they were fully aware that very soon they had to get down to the business of sorting out the political future of Pacific America. The Nootka Convention was a broad agreement. Now Vancouver and Bodega y Quadra had to discuss it and settle its specific terms.

The Spanish were well prepared. One of the first actions of the new viceroy of Mexico, Conde de Revilla Gigedo, had been to send a naval expedition as far as Alaska. Following the signing of the Nootka Sound Convention, Gigedo was instructed to establish exclusive territory at the Strait of Juan de Fuca with a border to run northward up to Cook Inlet at approximately 60°. While this would give Britain exclusive control over the whole of Nootka Sound, it would preserve the vast expanse of inland territories for the Spanish Crown. Spain had also concluded that the maintenance of a garrison and village at Friendly Cove was too costly and that the land should be ceded to the British. Armed with this information and the depositions from the various fur trade captains, Bodega y Quadra must have felt extremely confident in his future negotiations with Vancouver and in his ability to persuade him to accept these proposals.

Vancouver's position, however, was not so fortunate. The mail aboard the *Daedalus* had not brought any updated instructions for him. He was expected to hand over a copy of a letter from the Spanish first minister instructing Bodega y Quadra to hand back all British buildings and land in Nootka Sound as a mere formality.

Bodega y Quadra sent him a letter setting out Spain's position. It said that Meares's claims had to be false because no substantial buildings existed. Spain had nothing to hand over. Therefore, the two countries' differences could be resolved as soon as Vancouver accepted that Spanish sovereignty would extend from California to an international boundary at the Strait of Juan de Fuca. The British, the Americans, and the Russians could do what they wanted with the territory farther north. As soon as

Vancouver accepted these terms, Bodega y Quadra would immediately hand over Friendly Cove to him, including all the newly constructed buildings and fortifications.

Vancouver was shocked to read these terms. To him the proposals ran contrary to the Nootka Sound Convention. And he had received no instructions to discuss Spain's sovereignty of the coast, which, he understood, was to extend only as far north as had already been settled by the Spaniards, that is, only as far as San Francisco. He had no idea about what to do with Friendly Cove if it were handed over to him either.

Vancouver declined the offer, saying that his authority did not extend to such discussions. It was obvious that both governments had misunderstood the aim of the negotiations, one believing that Britain had settled them, the other that better terms could be negotiated. Talks began between the two men, but frustratingly and eventually, Bodega y Quadra granted to the British the small plot of land which Meares claimed to have purchased from Maquinna and upon which his shed had been built. On seeing it, Vancouver referred to it as "a small pittance of rocks and sandy beach". He found it hard to believe that this tiny area could possibly be considered "as the object of restitution expressed by the terms" of the convention between Britain and Spain. Convinced that a misunderstanding had occurred, he was taken to see Maquinna, who promptly called Meares a liar and told Vancouver that he had not sold any land to him.

Vancouver was now unsure as to how he and Bodega y Quadra should proceed. The dispatches he had been sending to the British government and the Admiralty had met with no response. Increasingly frustrated by the vagueness of his instructions, Vancouver decided to send his first lieutenant, Zachary Mudge, to London to seek clarification. He would have a long wait.

When the two men first had met, Bodega y Quadra had asked Vancouver to name some prominent landmark for both men jointly. Much later, Vancouver suggested that the enormous island that they were on should be named "Quadra and Vancouver" as a mark of their negotiations. Perhaps this was a subtle way for Vancouver to save face and a means of staking Britain's claim on the region. In later years, as Spanish influence waned, the name was shortened to Vancouver Island.

On 22 September, nearly a month after his meetings with Vancouver began, Bodega y Quadra sailed for California. Vancouver remained for an additional month and decided to carry out surveys. By October, with the summer season now at an end and the weather worsening, Vancouver left Nootka Sound and sailed to Alta, California, reconnoitring Spanish defences along the coastline. He had also arranged another meeting with Bodega y Quadra in Monterey, still hoping to find communications from his government that would help him resolve the problems he had encountered. There was no news, but Vancouver sent copies of his charts, correspondence, and dispatches to London, choosing Lieutenant Broughton to be his courier.

Broughton arrived back in England in the summer of 1793 within a month of Zachary Mudge. Both were to discover that a lot had changed. In April 1792, war had broken out in Europe with France declaring war on Austria. The republicans had been intent on overthrowing the French monarchy, and on 20 June 1791, King Louis and Marie Antoinette had fled unsuccessfully from Paris. They were arrested at Varennes and imprisoned. Later both would be executed by guillotine.

Bidding farewell to Bodega y Quadra, who went to Mexico, Vancouver set off to explore the Sandwich Islands, arriving in February 1793. Returning to the Northwest Coast, Vancouver continued his surveying programme. At Friendly Cove in October, he was told that no dispatches had been received from the British government. By now exhausted and sick, and with the weather worsening again, Vancouver decided to sail south to warmer climes. In San Francisco, he first learned of the guillotining of the king and queen of France and the turmoil that was raging through Europe. He pressed on to Monterey, and then San Diego. After a survey of Baja, he set off again to the Sandwich Islands.

Back home in Britain, the second Nootka Convention had been signed on 12 February 1793. In it, Spain had promised to provide an indemnity of 210,000 Spanish dollars against Meares's claim for $653,433 for the damages suffered by him and his partners.

In March 1794, after completing a survey of some of the islands, Vancouver departed for the final time and sailed directly to Cook Inlet, Alaska, from where he planned to sail southward in a final attempt to find the North-West Passage. By now the crew were feeling low, and Vancouver's health was beginning to suffer in the freezing temperatures, ice floes, and violent storms. He completed his final survey on 19 August 1794, naming his anchorage Port Conclusion. Sailing into Nootka Sound for one final visit on 2 September, Vancouver met Spain's new governor of Friendly Cove, José Manuel de Álava. He was friendly and hospitable towards Vancouver but had no new instructions for him, although he did tell him that a ship was due to arrive any day and it was possible that it might be bringing news from Britain as well as instructions for Álava, who had now been tasked with completing the negotiations with Vancouver following the death of Bodega y Quadra.

Vancouver therefore agreed to stay on, but by now his men were almost driven mad with their impatience to return home. By mid-October, with no sign of the ship, Vancouver and Álava decided to depart for Monterey, where they hoped belated instructions might await them. It had now been two and a half years since Vancouver had heard anything from Britain.

On 12 November, Álava did receive instructions. He was able to tell Vancouver that the British and Spanish courts had at last come to an amicable understanding of Article One of the Nootka Sound Convention. Ironically, the conflagration in Europe had brought Britain and Spain together as allies, and the intention of the agreement was to allow both nations to save face. An adjustment had been agreed upon on, as Vancouver later wrote, "nearly on the terms which I had so repeatedly offered to Senr. Quadra in September of 1792".

The Third Nootka Convention, entitled the "Convention for the Mutual Abandonment of Nootka", had been signed by the British and Spanish negotiators in Madrid on 11 January 1794.

Meares's land would be handed over to Britain; Spain would dismantle their forts and village; a British flag would be raised and lowered; and then both nations would abandon the Sound, which would then be left under the control of the natives. Although it would remain open to ships of any nation, none of them would be allowed to establish a permanent base there.

Richard's reaction to these decisions is unknown, but I suspect that he had resigned himself to the fact that his dream of establishing a profitable trading establishment at Nootka was now over and his thoughts were turning to the amount of compensation the British government would be able to obtain from Spain.

But the ceremony of cession would not be carried out by Vancouver.

A new commissioner had been appointed by the British government. His name was Lieutenant Thomas Pearce. In the uniform of His Majesty's Royal Marines, as commissioner of Great Britain, he was to instigate a formal settlement.

Upon hearing this news, and now that his survey of the coast had been completed, Vancouver considered that the government was not expecting him to stay any longer in the Pacific. On 2 December 1794, *Discovery* and *Chatham* began their homeward journey by way of Cape Horn, thereby completing a circumnavigation of North America.

On 16 March 1795, while the *Discovery* and *Chatham* were visiting Valparaiso, Álava and Pearce sailed northward from Monterey to Friendly Cove. They disembarked from their ships for a few days, conducted interviews, raised and lowered the British flag, and presented official documents to Maquinna which outlined their agreement which he was to show to future traders. Álava then ordered the Spanish fortifications to be dismantled and valuable items stored in his ship. Then they left, the local people staring at the retreating vessel.

Aftermath

Vancouver arrived in England on 20 October 1795. He faced almost overwhelming difficulties upon his return home, perhaps the worst arising from the behaviour of Thomas Pitt, the 2nd Baron Camelford, whom Vancouver had severely disciplined during the voyage for various indiscretions and had eventually sent home in disgrace. But there were other problems: Banks was particularly vindictive towards him, especially over the publication of his memoirs, and his accomplishments were not given the recognition they deserved—which would remain the case throughout his lifetime.

Vancouver went to live in Petersham, because of the magnificent view from Richmond Hill, but his health, never good at the best of times, was deteriorating. He died in obscurity on 10 May 1798, perhaps of kidney failure or perhaps because of a hyperthyroid condition. This was only three years after he had completed an epic voyage and was still at work on his memoirs. He is buried at St Peter's Church, Petersham.

George Vancouver's grave

The Fate of John Meares

The Meares Memorial and its subsequent presentation to Parliament on 13 May 1790 had ushered Meares into the limelight. His document had served William Pitt's purpose extremely well in his campaign to halt Spanish incursion into the North Pacific and gain control of the sea. But once the Nootka Crisis had been settled and Britain's head turned to face other problems emanating from Europe, Meares soon became forgotten.

He soon disappeared from public view, but he still had some issues to be resolved arising from the Nootka trade. For example, on 30 July 1792, Richard and John Meares wrote a letter to the diplomat Sir Ralph Woodford asking whether a decision had been made about the transportation of some sea otter furs to Peking (Beijing). It seems that the East India Company was procrastinating over their valuation. And as the *Hindostan*, the vessel that would be taking them, was departing within a few days, any further delay would lead to "disagreeable consequences".

Woodford wrote to the government the following day asking about their position. On 7 September, he replied, transmitting an offer from the East India Company to buy the 1,150 sea otter furs at 8 guineas per skin, which amounted to £9,660. On 11 September, Richard and Meares accepted the offer, but the following day they wrote to Woodford asking him to take their complaint to the foreign secretary, Lord Grenville, which was that only extreme distress had obliged them to accept the offer.

It is believed that Meares eventually returned to his first love, which was the sea and active duty in the Royal Navy. On 26 February 1795, he was rewarded for his role in the Nootka Crisis by being promoted to commander and receiving a considerable increase in his pay. He was also given the title of baronet, which meant that he could be called Sir John Meares.

In 1794 Meares had applied to the British Admiralty for funds arising out of the Nootka Crisis, but so far as is known, he received none of the indemnity money paid by Spain. On 12 May 1796, he wrote to Evan Nepean at the British Admiralty saying that while on "impress duty" in Ireland, he had suffered an injury but had now sufficiently recovered to request an assignment to active duty.

Meares always regarded the city of Bath as his spiritual home. He died there on 29 January 1809, probably at the age of fifty-three. The cause of his death is not known. In his will, he stated that he owned property in Jamaica, but the value when probated was estimated to be under £7,500. He lists a brother and sister as unnamed beneficiaries, but there is no reference to his wife, Mary Ann Guilliband, whom he had married in 1796. Most likely she had predeceased him.

The will also lists several people who he claimed owed him money. One of these was Daniel Beale, a partner in the Etches Company, who supposedly owed him £21,600 "under an arbitration". Another, James Drummond, supposedly owed him £10,783. But these claims were not included in Meares's overall worth when the will was proved on 19 April 1809.

Meares was criticised in some quarters for his claim of damages of $653,433 in the Nootka negotiations for himself and the Etches Company, citing the fact that the financial losses caused by the seizure of his ships by Spain were not that great. His claim, though, included what would be treated today as punitive damages. For he suffered not only the loss of his ships but also his dream of establishing a permanent fur trading enterprise between the Northwest Coast and China. Most probably the amount of

210,000 Spanish dollars, which Spain had settled on for Britain in 1793, was close to the mark. A document on file at the National Archives, Kew shows that this was the amount that Ralph Woodford had signed a receipt from Spain for. Another file indicates that Meares felt he might have been victimised by the Etches sponsors in the settlement. He warned the Admiralty during negotiations that he still had outstanding claims against that enterprise. The Nootka Crisis had caused a bitter fallout among the partners of the Associated Merchants.

The *Butterworth* Squadron

Just at Vancouver's ships were preparing to leave Falmouth on 1 April 1791, the *Butterworth* squadron was getting ready to sail from London. This expedition was comprised of three British owned vessels, *Butterworth*, *Jackal*, and *Prince Lee Boo*, that had been financed by a company of merchants led by Sir William Curtis, a member of Parliament who was a fervent supporter of Pitt and his bellicose stance against Spain.

Curtis's company had been granted a monopoly for trade on the Northwest Coast, replacing John Meares and the Etches family.

William was the son of Joseph Curtis of Wapping, a baker of ship's biscuits, who was an excellent example of a person from humble origins who had made good in the City. He became a successful banker and later a friend of George IV, even accompanying him on a visit to Scotland. In 1795, Curtis became mayor of London.

Curtis was likeable, convivial, and very overweight, as well as being an unconscious buffoon. He was often characterised as the "City Gourmandiser" or in Highland dress as "Wandering Willie".

It is unclear whether Richard was in any way financially involved in the *Butterworth* squadron as it was known. It is highly likely that the two men knew each other as both had a strong presence in the City. A naturalist, Sigismund Bacstrom, the surgeon for the expedition, had previously sailed with Joseph Banks, and as we have seen, Banks was a close friend of Richard.

BONNIE WILLIE.

Sir William Curtis

During 1791, as the Nootka Convention was being agreed, Curtis was actively involved in discussions with the East India Company and the South Sea Company about opening the monopolies that would now be afforded to British traders. Despite Bacstrom's letter to Joseph Banks in August of that year in which he claimed that the *Butterworth* venture was only interested in bringing back "valuable drugs or natural products" and was fully "independent of the new fur trade between Nootka and China", no evidence was shown that it was involved in anything other than the lucrative maritime fur trade and the seal factory of Tierra del Fuego.

Richard was aware of the *Butterworth* project from the very beginning, but in view of what had happened at Nootka, and because his five-year licences with the East India Company and the South Sea Company had expired, very possibly Richard had decided to concentrate on his other interests.

Trading sea otter pelts with the Chinese had not proved as profitable as he had imagined. Only the Russians seemed to be able to make money at it. Later correspondence reveals that Richard and Meares still had issues to be resolved arising from the Nootka trade. Also there seems to have been a falling-out between the directors of the company with Daniel Beale taking legal action against Meares and Richard for money he claimed he was owed by them.

It was time for Richard to move on.

CHAPTER 6

RICHARD THE FOREIGN AGENT

At the outbreak of the French Revolution in 1789 and later the Napoleonic Wars, obtaining information about the enemy's plans was principally carried out by diplomats who would report their findings to the Foreign Office. Like the Home Office and the Admiralty, the Foreign Office also ran secret agents. The Admiralty's main concern was to assess the state of readiness of the French warships in the north-western bases. The captains of British vessels whose warships were docked in the French ports were instructed to observe and report. But sightings of enemy ship activity and movements could just as easily emanate from sources other than agents, such as fishermen, smugglers, and merchants who traded with the Continent.

As an importer of wine, brandy, and tea, Richard was a merchant whose business was dependent on speedy, accurate information from abroad, especially from the Continent, to which he often travelled. His base in the City of London was well-situated to keep abreast of events. He would no doubt frequent Lloyd's Coffee House, which has been described as "a hotbed of commercial gossip and news".

How or exactly when Richard became a British agent is sadly unknown. Did he approach the government, or did the government approach him? Curiously, in 1783, two years before he involved himself in the sea otter trade, he had been recruited into the services of Catherine II, Empress of Russia, and had been given the sum of £2,000 to purchase a private yacht and a commission in the Russian navy. The amount of £2,000 would be worth around £300,000 today.

This came at a time when Russia and England were not on friendly terms. Russia was expanding its territories at an alarming rate. Crimea was annexed from the Turks, and then through the acquisition of the territories of the Crimean khanate, which extended from the Caucasus Mountains to the Bug River in south-western Russia, Russia held the north shore of the Black Sea and was in a position to threaten the existence of the Ottoman Empire and to establish a foothold in the Mediterranean. Catherine also sought to renew the alliance with Austria—Turkey's neighbour and enemy—and she renounced her alliance with Prussia and England, who were alarmed by Russia's ambitions.

In his memoirs, Richard makes no reference at all to his role in the Russian Navy nor any to this period in his life. It is also possible that he was already a British agent and had been allowed to work for Russia with the government's blessing. By 1785 he certainly was working as a secret agent, but at that time the British secret service was little more than a small surveillance operation headed by Evan Nepean at the Home Office.

I refer to the postscript of Richard's letter to Nathaniel Portlock dated 3 September 1785:

> I have omitted to mention that you are particularly required not to let slip any possible opportunity of sending intelligence of your proceedings from the time you leave the English Channel until your return to England; you are to address such dispatches to Richard Cadman Etches, London and enclose them, under cover, to George Rose Esq., at The treasury, London.

Although unusual, it was not considered outlandish for an Englishman to leave his country to work in Russia. Samuel Bentham, a brother of the philosopher Jeremy, on realising that his opportunities for promotion from a shipwright apprentice in the Chatham dockyard would not be easy, decided to join the Russian army. He designed and built galleys for the Russian navy and fought with distinction against the Turks in the Battle of Kherson in June 1788, ending up with the rank of brigadier general. Returning to England, he was not only warmly welcomed but also appointed inspector general of naval works, reporting directly to the Admiralty Board.

By 1789, Richard, who sometimes used the alias of Andrew Smith or R. Ellis, was still working for Catherine. Now his current role becomes clearer. He was employed as the commissary general of her marine at the ports of Glückstadt on the River Elbe and Ostend in the Austrian Netherlands, responsible for the coast from Ostend to Copenhagen. The Commissiart Department is "a government organisation responsible for supplies and provisions for the army, as ordered by the secretary of state for war but reporting to the Treasury". A commissary in this context is an officer who has been delegated by a superior to carry out this function. Richard had been given charge of several armed vessels with which to "cruise against the Swedes and Turks", with whom Russia was then at war.

During the Russo-Swedish War of 1788–1790, Richard had organised a flotilla of Russian privateers to sail under English captains in the Baltic. Ironically, Sir Sidney Smith, of whom there will be more later, was fighting on the side of the Swedes in the same war.

The correspondence of Sir James Burges, who was undersecretary of state for foreign affairs from 1789 to 1790, reveals that while in the employment of Catherine II, Richard devised several ideas for the promotion of Russia's interests, including one for the capture of Bassora, the old name for Basra, which he described as "this grand Emporium of Commerce" whose possession, he maintained, would open up worldwide commerce for Russia, including the Americas and the Pacific.

In early September of 1789, Richard had received information that three Turkish merchants had purchased a large quantity of goods and merchandise containing certain items which were prohibited under the laws of the armed neutrality. The cargo had been laden aboard a vessel called the *Isabella*, which at the time was laying under English colours—that is flying the English flag—in Hamburg, from where the three merchants intended to sail.

Richard ordered an armed Russian galley called the *Krudnor*, commanded by Captain David Williams, and a Russian cruiser called *Woronzow*, commanded by Alexander Carr, to keep a lookout for the *Isabella* as they followed her to sea. If she were found, their instructions were to board her in the name of Catherine, Empress of Russia, and to carry her to the port of Ostend, where they were to inspect her cargo in detail, a task not feasible at sea, and then await further orders from Richard.

The *Isabella*, after having been found by *Krudnor* on 14 September, was boarded and then escorted into the port of Ostend. Her captain, George McKilligin, delivered her papers and the accounts of her cargo to Sir John Peters, who was Britain's consul at Ostend, for examination. Then, at Alexander Carr's request, they were deposited with the judge of the Court of Admiralty there.

It was not long afterwards that Richard arrived to claim the Turkish merchants and their cargoes as legal prizes on behalf of the empress. However, the judge at the Court of Admiralty had ruled that before any such action could be taken, Richard's commission had first to be recognised as being acceptable to the laws of the Netherlands. He was therefore obliged to apply to Le Conte Trautsmandorf, the prime minister of the court of Brussels. Recognising Richard's authority, Trautsmandorf allowed him to return to Ostend to carry out his duty. Richard assured Captain McKilligin that he was only concerned with that portion of the cargo that belonged to the Turks and was not intending to claim the vessel *Isabella* as part of Russia's prize. He even gave his word that all other parts of the cargo would be "sacredly preserved" and that McKilligin would be paid his full freight for the Turks' cargo, plus demurrage and all other expenses that had been incurred from the point at which *Isabella*'s course had been altered. He also made it clear that McKilligin should under no circumstance be deprived of the command of his ship. Nor had he any intention of insulting His Majesty's flag, which had continued to fly during the whole time that *Isabella* had been anchored at Ostend, nor the captain, his officers, or his crewmen.

By now Richard was anxious to remove the Turks' cargo and to allow the *Isabella* to continue her journey with the remainder of her cargo. However, he discovered that under an ordinance passed during the American War of Independence, no part of any cargo claimed as a prize could be landed on the dock at Ostend or come to that, at any other port in the Netherlands. Richard was therefore advised to hire a vessel and to have the Turks' cargo transferred directly to it. In addition, he was required to return to Brussels to sort out the legality of the prize.

While he was away, a British sloop of war arrived and anchored off

Ostend. Her officers immediately ordered Alexander Carr and his Russian crew, who were now based aboard the *Isabella*, to disembark. The men went ashore, and the ship immediately sailed out of Ostend in the same condition as she had arrived.

Sometime afterwards, Captain McKilligin approached the British commissioners of Oyez, Terminer, and Gaol delivery for the jurisdiction of the Court of Admiralty to have Richard charged with "felony and piracy". He managed to procure a warrant for his arrest.

Eventually David Williams, commander of the *Krudnor*, was committed to the New Prison at Tothill Fields, Bridewell, and later removed to Newgate. Joseph Armstrong, the ship's carpenter, was sent to Clerkenwell.

Richard does not appear to have been arrested, probably because he was based abroad. To clear his name, in 1790 he and his lawyers drew up a petition for "a Bill to pass the Great Seal for a Free Pardon for Piracy" in which he set out the circumstances which had led to his involvement with the *Isabella*.

The petition was followed up with an affidavit sworn by him on 22 March 1791 before John Boydell, Lord Mayor of London. The affidavit restates the wording of the piracy petition, but it strongly denies certain accusations that had been made against Richard. Richard states that at no time had he made any application to any country with whom Britain was at war, such as the USA, France, Spain, or Holland, or any foreign state or court for letters of marque against any British vessel.

A letter of marque was a government licence that authorised a person usually known as a privateer or corsair to attack and capture enemy vessels. Once a vessel was captured, the privateer could then bring the case of that prize before his own admiralty court for the condemnation and transfer of ownership to the privateer.

Richard denies being a foreign agent by affirming that he "never did directly or indirectly carry out any communication or correspondence with or give any Information or Intelligence to any Minister, Agent or Subject of any Foreign State Court or Power at War with Great Britain".

He also declares that he never had any interest, shares, or concerns in any ships or vessels under the British flag or any other flag as owner, agent, husband, or director, except in a vessel named the *Golden Eagle*, which was fitted out at Portsmouth during the American War of Independence. On her second voyage, the *Golden Eagle* was captured in the Bay of Biscay by an American letter of marque and carried to Bilbao. The story behind this is an interesting one.

The *Golden Eagle* was one of dozens of British merchant ships captured at sea by an American privateer named Jonathan Haraden. Preying on the British fear of privateers, he managed to outmanoeuvre much larger enemies, often capturing them without firing a shot. As soon as Haraden ordered his helmsman to steer towards a vessel, his crew automatically assumed that their prize was in the bag.

In early April 1780, Haraden set sail aboard the *General Pickering* bound for Bilbao, carrying a cargo of sugar. Bilbao was a favourite rendezvous for privateers. In the Bay of Biscay, Haraden overtook the *Golden Eagle*, which had twenty-two guns and sixty men. Seeing it was dark, Haraden decided to bluff. "This is an American frigate, sir," he shouted through his speaking trumpet. "Surrender, or I will strike you with a broadside."

The *Golden Eagle* fell for the ruse and surrendered. Haraden placed fifteen of his men on board and sailed into Bilbao with his prize captured alongside him. But another ship was sailing out: the *Achilles*, a British privateer with 42 guns and 140 men. At dusk it took back the *Golden Eagle*. Haraden was not one to give up easily though.

By morning, word broke out that a British privateer and an American privateer were about to do battle—within sight of land. Thousands flocked to the coast and got closer to the action in fishing boats, cutters, rowboats, and sailing vessels.

Harden manoeuvred the *General Pickering* between the *Achilles* and a line of shoals and raked the British vessel with broadside fire. The wind died down, so it took two hours for the *Achilles* to work herself in position and escape the powerful American fire. The *General Pickering*, with her cargo of sugar, sat so low in the water that the larger ship was unable to rake her. A witness said that the *General Pickering* looked like a longboat next to a ship. Another said that Haraden stood exposed as shot flew around him as if he were amid a shower of snowflakes.

Cheers rose from the flotilla of boats and the spectators on shore as the *General Pickering* raked the *Achilles*. Finally, the *Achilles* captain was able to bring the ship about and return fire on the *General Pickering*.

After three hours, the *General Pickering* had run short of ammunition. Haraden then ordered his men to load the cannons with crowbars. Flying like arrows, the crowbars tore through the *Achilles*'s rigging, smashed into the decks, and sent the gun crews running from their stations. The torrent of crowbars had persuaded the *Achilles*'s captain to retreat, allowing the *General Pickering* to recapture the *Golden Eagle*.

By now the flotilla of small boats had surrounded the *General Pickering*. At the close of battle, they escorted the ship into the harbour. The crowd swarmed to his landing place, caught up Captain Haraden, and carried him through the streets on their shoulders.

The grateful owners of the *General Pickering* gave Haraden an engraved silver hot-chocolate pot and two silver cans, which are now kept in the Peabody Essex Museum in Salem. Jonathan Haraden died in Salem on 23 November 1803.

Richards ends his affidavit concerning the accusation of piracy against him with a reference to a comment about him that had appeared in *The Gazetteer* on Thursday, 27 May 1790, which read:

> It is said that one of the persons chiefly interested in the Affair of Nootka Sound and on whose respectable authority Ministers have so rashly and publicly committed the English Nation did in the course of the last war make Application to the Court of France for letters of Marque to cruise against the British Trade which from his utmost knowledge he could materially affect: it is certainly worth the attention of Parliament to enquire whether Ministers have listened to the Testimony of any such Character—it is in our Power to be more explicit.

Richard asserted that the comments were false and scandalous, having been inserted by a "wicked and malicious person" who had a desire to injure his character and reputation. The nature of these comments is unknown, but according to the correspondence of Sir James Lamb, in January 1790 the Foreign Office was provided with full knowledge of Richard's plans when the captain of one of his Russian privateers succumbed to a bribe of £50 and handed over a box containing his private papers to the British consul in Ostend. Whatever was contained in that box was obviously not treasonable.

Richard's affidavit was sent to the office of Evan Nepean by his brother William. In his covering letter, William bemoans the lack of a decision by the government as to whether Richard is to be pardoned in respect of "his late lamented connexion with Russia" and asks whether there is any obstacle preventing a pardon from being granted. He adds that should "every atrocious report" made against his brother be the reason why the pardon is not being granted, then he begs permission to speak to Evan Nepean within a few days and asks Nepean to read the enclosed affidavit.

The pardon had obviously been referred to the Home Department, where, from 1782 to 1794, Evan Nepean was the undersecretary of state. Nothing further is on record.

The British Secret Service

With the outbreak of the French Revolutionary War on 1 February 1793, and with the Aliens Act, which monitored the entry of people into Britain, especially the hundreds of French émigrés who came flocking into London, having become law on 7 January 1793, the small surveillance unit headed by Evan Nepean which he had set up soon after his appointment would quickly expand into the Alien Office. The surveillance unit was still active in 1792, now conducted by William Clarke with twelve assistants. For the duration of the war, the Alien Office was run by William Wickham. Known by the title of "the Master Spy", Wickham was an expert linguist. His operation dealt with home security as well as espionage on the Continent. Later he would be based in Switzerland and control Britain's continental espionage set-up.

It is possible that Richard had been appointed as one of Nepean's agents in 1790, and his brief was to procure foreign intelligence. As part of his pardon, Richard may have been given a special role by Nepean. Richard had already amassed a detailed knowledge of North Sea and Baltic ports, acquired during his time working for Catherine, and this was made available to British authorities.

Sir Evan Nepean

However, because of Richard's long involvement with Russia, Nepean initially had put him on probation. He was watched by William Clarke, as was the Russian ambassador. However, there is no evidence that Richard was a double agent. In his letter to Evan Nepean mentioned earlier, William Etches refers to Richard's "late lamented connexion with Russia". So, it must be that the relationship was over.

The French Revolution had initially been supported by many Britons, but its aftermath had caused them to look across the Channel with a great deal of trepidation and wonder whether it would affect them. Because of the turbulence it had created, it was impossible for an Englishman to enter France with any degree of safety. For this reason, Richard had decided to become a Danish citizen. He had probably achieved this in Copenhagen in 1789. This enabled him to flit in and out of Europe, especially France, with impunity. He soon became acquainted with French ministers and dignitaries in Paris. He felt that "far more might be effected with the French government by private, rather than by public negotiation".

His ability to enter the Temple Prison in Paris at will, without even leaving a nom de guerre, made him at one time a candidate for the title of the Scarlet Pimpernel. I have been told by a local historian in Ashbourne that Baroness Orczy visited Ashbourne in 1901, presumably researching for her novel, but I have not been able to verify this.

On 1 February 1793, France declared war on Britain, and six days later they declared war on Spain. On 13 February, the First Coalition was formed involving Britain, Austria, Prussia, the Netherlands, Sardinia-Piedmont, and Spain. The Aliens Act of 1793, mentioned earlier, was prompted by the unrest in France.

One of France's major strategies was to attempt to isolate Britain from any commercial dealings with the continent of Europe. As part of this plan, France resisted any attempts by the British government to obtain the release of those merchant seamen who had been captured by French soldiers at the outset of the war.

Naturally, this was totally unacceptable to the British government, which had employed strenuous efforts to secure the release of all prisoners.

Sir William Eden, afterwards Lord Auckland, went to Dieppe in May 1795 to propose an exchange of sailors, but the National Convention, which was the parliament of the French Revolution, would only consent to the exchange of naval officers. With the support of Evan Nepean, Richard submitted a proposal to Lord Spencer in which he stated that, at his own expense, he was prepared to journey to Paris to see if he could secure the release of the prisoners, who by now numbered twelve thousand.

Richard's proposal was accepted. In the summer of 1795, he arrived in Paris to begin his negotiations. His influence and ability were such that he managed to persuade the Convention to agree to his securing an exchange of prisoners at a total expense of about £600. Richard achieved this without any involvement or interference from either government.

13 Vendémiare (5 October 1795)

Unfortunately, Richard says that he suffered a serious injury while in Paris, having found himself a spectator of the dreadful carnage that ensued when Napoleon ordered the cannonade of the people who were marching on the Convention. This event was known as 13 Vendémiare in the calendar of the French Republic.

The French Revolution had created many social reforms which were welcomed by the populace, but the government's anti-Catholic attitude was anathema to the fiercely Catholic Vendée region. Resentment here led to the formation of a rebel army known as the Chouans. They managed to defeat several revolutionary armies, but on 22 December 1793 at the Battle of Savenay, their rebellion was virtually quashed.

While most of the Chouans accepted the offer of an amnesty, a small contingent of royalists and fanatics continued to offer resistance. They suffered additional defeats and setbacks, but with the support of the British in the form of four thousand émigrés, British soldiers, cannons, muskets, food, and clothing, they began to march on Paris at the beginning of October 1795.

Fully aware of the danger they faced, the Convention decided to remain in their meeting rooms until the crisis was resolved. Troops were mustered to defend the attack, but they numbered only five thousand, compared with the royalists, whose army had thirty thousand men. On 4 October, the National Guard made a feeble attempt to put down the unrest. Their commander, General Menou, was forced invite the royalists to discuss the terms under which they would disperse.

Sensing Menou's approach as a sign of weakness, the royalists encouraged others to rise with them. Realising his mistake, Menou launched a cavalry attack. Although it temporarily cleared the royalists, the Convention decided to relieve him of his command. They appointed Paul-François Barras as his replacement.

A young general named Napoleon Bonaparte arrived at the Convention to see what was happening. He was quickly ordered to join the forces that Barras was gathering. He agreed but insisted that he be given complete freedom of movement. Barras was happy to let him take control. Napoleon promptly ordered his men to retrieve forty cannons that were located nearby. A probing attack by the royalists in the early morning of 5 October was repulsed, but a few hours later they began their major assault. Napoleon had arranged his cannons in commanding areas with effective fields of fire. Although the republican forces were outnumbered 6 to 1, the advancing royalist ranks were cut down by the grapeshot that was fired into them.

Despite having had his horse shot from under him, Napoleon survived the ordeal of the two-hour engagement and was completely unscathed. The power of the cannons had forced the royalist advance to waver, giving Napoleon the chance to order a counterattack, which resulted in about three hundred royalists lying dead on the streets of Paris. This night, later to be referred to as 13 Vendémiare, brought an end to the royalist threat to the Convention. The Scottish philosopher and historian Thomas Carlyle later said that Napoleon had given his opponents "a whiff of grapeshot". Napoleon now became a national hero. His career prospered.

Although he was only present as a spectator, at some point in the battles, Richard claims, he was seriously injured. He does not elaborate in his memoirs, but perhaps he too suffered from "a whiff of grapeshot". The injury did not dampen Richard's commercial spirit, though, because soon afterwards he went to Holland and set up as a merchant.

Napoleon firing at Royalist Forces

The Attack on England, 1795

His memoirs state that while in Holland, Richard discovered that all the small craft throughout the Seven United Provinces which made up the republic had been requisitioned for the transportation of a large French army, under the command of a General Bournonville, to the Essex and Suffolk coasts. The French were aware that the British defences along this part of the coastline were sadly lacking. Having made landfall, the French army planned to march on to attack London.

I cannot trace a General Bournonville, but I believe that the general in question may have been Pierre de Ruel, who was the Marquis of Beurnoville. But this is of little relevance here.

In the light of his discovery, Richard visited all the Dutch ports and made an inventory of all the requisitioned craft, taking note of their tonnage and generally observing the state of readiness the craft were in for the intended sortie into England.

This done, Richard set sail for England in a fishing boat so that he could not only apprise the British government of the French threat but also put forward his suggestions on how the threat could be averted.

The Lords of the Admiralty apparently adopted Richard's ideas straightaway. An armament commanded by Admiral Sir Richard Bickerton, as chief naval officer, and Captain Lieutenant Charles Doyle, as chief military officer, was fitted out and set sail in HMS *Ramilies* for Texel, an island in the northern part of the Netherlands. Richard went with the ship as a volunteer.

The plan was to deliver a surprise attack and entice the fleet into view. But, presumably, the sight of HMS *Ramilies* was enough to deter the enemy as no engagement took place. According to Dawson and Hobson, "It was in great measure through [Richard's] instructions that the French project of invasion fell to the ground."

In December 1795 Richard returned to Paris. From there he was able to reveal to the British government at home the real purpose of the immense naval and military preparations that were being undertaken in France, which had for so long been kept a profound secret.

According to the French thinking, Britain's East India possessions would be most vulnerable to attack via Egypt. The British government, though, had received subsequent information which they considered to be more reliable than that provided by Richard, but the landing of Napoleon and his army some months afterwards in Aboukir Bay, his movements from there to Alexandria and Damietta, his ascending the Nile to Cairo, and his intention of proceeding to the cities of Ginnah and Corsire on the Red Sea finally convinced the government of the accuracy of Richard's details. As we shall see later, Sir Sidney Smith was involved in the Battle of Aboukir as an adviser to the Turkish army.

The practicality of transporting an army from the coasts of the Red

Sea to India may be doubted, but Richard was an eyewitness to many large ships in the French ports which were being transferred to Americans who were appointed to take command of them.

These ships were manned by Americans but also had British prisoners provided with certificates stating that they too were Americans. The plan was for the ships to sail under American colours around the Cape of Good Hope, where they were to rendezvous at the French islands in the Indian Ocean and await the arrival of the French army. From there the ships were to proceed up the Red Sea to the port of Corsire and to transport the army to the coast of Malabar. But the failure of the French expedition in Egypt meant that further employment of this fleet was rendered unnecessary.

A Plan for Communicating Marine Intelligence, 1796

On 7 May 1796, Richard, who had recently returned from France, wrote to Earl Spencer, First Lord of the Admiralty:

> Upon my return from France I may be engaged in the employ of another department in communicating intelligence from that country with which I conceive my services for at which your lordship presides may be coupled to advantage.
>
> Confident from the authority I possess of the marine minister of that country for visiting Brest, L'Orient, Rockefort, Toulon and all the different ports for the purchasing of prize vessels, and being allowed the privilege of English seamen to navigate them, I am confident that I can organise and conduct an important system of communicating intelligence for the information of your lordship and the commanding officers of the respective stations on the coast of France, which no other person can have the authority or power of understanding.
>
> Exclusive of the importance of obtaining a supply of seamen from the prisoners of France, for His Majesty's service even without any exchange, but from confidence from my connections in that country, I am fully persuaded that if properly authorised in the capacity of a private individual of

not only renewing the exchange but of continuing it during the war.

No. 19 Bryanston St., Portman Square
Saturday, 7 May 1796
ENCLOSURE: A Plan of Communicating Marine Intelligence

First, to visit in person the ports of Havre, Cherbourg, St. Malo, Marlaix and Brest; at the latter to purchase one or more vessels and give orders for their equipment and for prisoners to navigate them. While this is conducting, to visit a second or third port as L'Orient, Nantes ... make my observations and return to Brest to dispatch the vessels preparing for sea etc., etc. (Perhaps it might be prudent to conceal the plan, to impress the crew and send the vessels home with seamen from the fleet) and afterwards to run to England with my observations.

Being allowed by the minister to authorise agents for the same purpose, together with my connections with most of the residents consuls at the ports of France and Holland, and by means of colouring my real views with all the publicity of a commercial speculation, I am confident that I can conduct and extend the plan, to all ports of France and Holland, at a mere trifling expenditure compared with the importance of the measure.

Richard Cadman Etches

Richard had developed an effective cover ploy for his trips to France. As an accredited purchaser of prize vessels, he had been given access to all the French ports. A cartel system existed under which the ships he purchased could be used for the exchange of prisoners of war; therefore, he had permission to use English seamen to sail them. In this letter he was proposing to gather marine intelligence which would be transferred to the Admiralty when his vessels were searched upon their return to his home port. He also suggested that the seamen could be impressed and the cartel system bypassed.

Spencer referred him to Evan Nepean, who by now was responsible for Admiralty intelligence. Soon Richard was providing naval and military intelligence from Holland as well as France.

Saving Sir Sidney Smith, 24 April 1798

Questions are often asked about the value of intelligence services. There is an assumption that intelligence gathering is nearly always costly; information that is obtained is untrustworthy and unverifiable; and it can be of little strategic or tactical value. Spies are often seen as deceitful, subversive double agents open to bribery and, at times, plainly corrupt.

This perception is nurtured because, by its very nature, espionage is clouded in secrecy, and successful operations cannot be publicised without revealing sources or putting operatives in danger. However, when things go wrong, the failure tends to seep quickly into the public domain—and opprobrium follows.

Sometimes, though, the details of a successful operation are revealed, the rescue of Sir Sidney Smith from the Temple Prison in Paris in April 1798 being a shining example. It was a complex and highly dangerous venture carried out almost entirely by the British secret service, one in which Richard Cadman Etches can be described as the mastermind. Yet in two major biographies of Sir Sidney Smith, Richard's name is not even mentioned, and both give much of the credit for the organisation and execution of the escape plot to French royalists.

This chapter will provide Richard with the credit he deserves.

Sir Sidney Smith

William Sidney Smith was born at Westminster on 21 June 1764, the second of three sons.

He was born into a military family. His father, John Smith, had been a captain in the Guards but had resigned his commission after the Battle of Minden, Germany. An Anglo-German army defeated the French in a major engagement on 1 August 1759 during the Seven Years War, but afterwards Smith was disgusted when his commander, Lord George

Germain, was censured and sent home for his refusal to carry out the orders of Ferdinand, Prince of Brunswick, who was in overall command.

While in Bath, John Smith had set his sights on an heiress, Mary Wilkinson, the daughter of an extremely rich merchant in the City of London. In 1760 he eloped with her. His father-in-law, having always regarded him as an adventurer and a rake, disinherited his daughter and severed all connection with her and the three sons she would later bear.

John Smith and Mary did not enjoy a happy relationship. Eventually, threatened by his violent behaviour, she fled back to Bath, installing the boys into a boarding school there. They were allowed to spend some time with their father, however, who had moved into a small cottage he had rented in Midgham, near Newbury, in Berkshire.

From an early age, Sidney, as he was known, showed remarkable qualities. He had a complete contempt for danger and a love of adventure, as well as an appetite for inventiveness and a dislike for authority. He carried these traits all through his distinguished career in the Royal Navy, becoming known for his recklessness in running into danger, coupled with his tremendous resourcefulness in escaping from it with great credit.

Sidney had a degree of education at Tonbridge and then Bath, but neither establishment could have contributed much to his career as, shortly before his twelfth birthday, he was appointed to HMS *Tortoise*.

Sidney owed much of this appointment to his father, a gentleman usher to Queen Charlotte, and to the Duke of Clarence, who later became his king and with whom Sidney would always remain on intimate terms.

To become an officer in the navy during the eighteenth century usually meant that the initial entry was largely by "interest". If a father knew a member of the Board of Admiralty or a serving admiral, he could obtain a King's Letter which would enable a young boy to be appointed as a captain's servant on a seagoing ship. In truth, these boys were not really servants but youngsters who wanted to make a life at sea their career.

The regulations provided that after six years at sea, the boys could be examined in seamanship for the rank of lieutenant. So, to gain time, boys were frequently entered into ships at an absurdly young age—in some cases as young as nine.

Sidney Smith as a young boy

The *Tortoise* was an armed store ship which was ordered to escort a convoy from Portsmouth to New York, but upon his return the following year, Smith was appointed to the brig *Unicorn*. It was here that he first experienced battle at sea. Off the US coast, the *Unicorn* chased the frigate *Raleigh* and fought a three-hour battle with her. The *Unicorn* suffered thirteen deaths and many wounded, including Smith, who was gashed by a splinter.

In September 1779 he was appointed to the *Sandwich*, the flagship of the Channel Fleet, and here he saw further action under the command of Admiral Sir George Rodney. A strong Spanish squadron had been sighted off the coast of St Vincent and was engaged in battle. The fighting lasted all night. Smith's alertness had been noted by the admiral.

Sidney Smith did not have to wait long for his first promotion. In September 1780, he was appointed to HMS *Alcide* as lieutenant, although his commission was not gazetted by the Admiralty for three years; almost certainly this was to conform to a regulation which prohibited any officer being so promoted until he had achieved the age of nineteen.

But even before confirmation of his lieutenancy had been made public, Smith was again promoted. Now he held the rank of commander on the

HMS Sloop *Fury*. And in October, just five years after he had initially joined the navy, he became captain of HMS *Alcmene*. In September 1783, Britain, France, and Spain signed the Treaty of Paris at Versailles recognising the independence of the United States of America. Smith continued to command HMS *Alcmene* until February 1784, when he arrived in Portsmouth and was paid off. In peacetime, like many officers, he found the navy too dull for his adventurous nature, so he decided to take advantage of an option given to unemployed officers, which was to travel abroad to learn languages. Smith chose to go to France despite his having been taught the language by his mother. The reason he gave for his decision was "of further qualifying myself for my country's service".

Setting off for Normandy, he spent two years in Caen, where he soon acquired a fluency in French. He made sure that he kept a sailor's weather eye open wherever he went. For example, he made a reconnaissance of the new naval harbour under construction at Cherbourg, basically a breakwater two and a half miles from the shore.

From France he went to Gibraltar, and from there to Morocco, to "spy out the land" and report his findings to the Admiralty.

Returning from his Mediterranean trip in the autumn of 1788, and with England still at peace, Smith soon became bored. He was no peacetime sailor and was hoping that trouble would break out somewhere.

When Catherine II of Russia and Joseph II of Austria jointly made war on the Ottoman Empire in 1790, Smith's prayers were answered, because King Gustav III of Sweden then seized the opportunity to attack Russia in the north. Despite not having the approval of the British government, Smith joined the king on 21 May as his principal naval adviser and as commander of a light squadron.

He made his impact at the Battle of Svensksund on 9–10 July by destroying a Russian blockade in the Bay of Viborg, causing them to lose sixty-four ships and over a thousand men. For his efforts, Gustav awarded Smith the Order of the Sword. The ceremony was performed by King George III himself on 16 May 1792. Smith was now permitted to use the title of Sir Sidney.

Sir Sidney Smith

On 29 March 1792, Gustav was assassinated. In France, the revolution was gaining momentum, the monarchy was about to fall, and war with Austria and Prussia was imminent. There was also concern about the Middle East, where the Ottoman Empire sat astride the British overland route to India. William Pitt, the prime minister, was determined that Britain should remain at peace no matter what transpired on the continent, but this did not affect Britain's espionage activity.

At the behest of Lord Grenville at the Foreign Office, Smith had been involved in preparing a confidential report about Russian and Turkish naval capabilities in the Black Sea area.

In June of 1791, King Louis XVI of France had attempted to escape but was intercepted at the border at Varennes and forced back to Paris, where, on 21 January 1793, he was executed. Less than a fortnight later, France declared war on Britain.

The French Revolution had by no means swept across the whole of the country. In some areas, notably the west, north-west, and south, there was great resistance to it. Lyons, Marseilles, and Toulon had declared for the royalists and had appealed to Britain for help. Learning while in Constantinople that the French naval base at Toulon was in the hands of the allies, Smith sailed off in a coaster named *Swallow* to offer his help to Lord Hood, commander of the Mediterranean Fleet.

But by the time of Smith's arrival in December 1793, the allies' position had become untenable and plans were being made to evacuate. Although Smith was an officer on half pay who held no official appointment in the Royal Navy, he was invited by Lord Hood as a guest on the *Victory*. Hood agreed with his suggestion that the military stores at the dockyard should be destroyed and that French ships which could not be withdrawn should be burnt. Smith was put in command of the units which took this action, but because of the pusillanimity of the supporting Spanish troops, the operation was only partially successful. Whereas Smith returned to England as a minor hero, in France he had created much bitterness. He was regarded as an arsonist who had acted outside the laws of war. In fact, Napoleon had even nicknamed him "Capitaine de Brulot".

Upon his return on 15 January 1794, the Admiralty gave Smith command of a frigate, *Diamond*, which was attached to the Channel Fleet. From this point onwards, Smith's secret service activities were undertaken on behalf of the Admiralty and the War Office and involved cloak-and-dagger operations arising out of revolutionary France and the European monarchies.

At the beginning of 1795, Smith was attached to a squadron of frigates under the command of Sir John Warren, commander of the Channel Fleet. His official orders included inshore operations against French merchant vessels, interception of neutral vessels, the capture of privateers, and the gathering of naval intelligence. But he also became involved in more clandestine activities. His intimate knowledge of the French coast and ports, and his fluency in the language, made it possible for him to create and sustain links between the British intelligence networks which were controlled from the Channel Islands and Switzerland and royalist counter-revolutionary forces.

On 9 February 1796, Smith left Spithead aboard *Diamond* under his usual orders to search for French privateers which preyed on British merchant shipping. One of them, a swift vessel called *Vengeur*, had evaded capture for several weeks. On 17 April, Smith found *Vengeur* sheltering close to Le Havre. He decided to set off in small boats to make a reconnaissance. Accompanying Smith were John Wesley Wright, who was his secretary aboard ship, and a French émigré, Jacques-Jean-Marie François Boudin de Tromelin.

As the boats neared *Vengeur*, a challenge was suddenly shouted from her deck, and quickly the boats ran alongside. Led by Smith, the party leapt aboard and engaged in hand-to-hand fighting on the deck. The French crew quickly surrendered. Smith, who had by now reached the cabins, requested that the officers do the same. But then it was discovered that one of the crew had cut the anchor cable and the ship was drifting into the mouth of the Seine.

There was hardly any wind, meaning that the *Diamond* could not be of any assistance. Nor could the small boats help to tow against the current. At daybreak, the alarm was sounded ashore, and soon French soldiers were rowed out from Le Havre. Smith prepared his men for hand-to-hand combat, but the French boats soon outnumbered the British. Some fierce fighting did follow, but it soon became obvious that the outcome was inevitable. Smith told his men that rescue from the *Diamond* was impossible and that their only option was to surrender.

Smith reluctantly handed over his sword to Captain Le Loup, the commander of the French boats that were encircling him and his men.

The Imprisonment of Sir Sidney Smith

The sight of the victorious French towing the recaptured *Vengeur* and the British boats into Le Havre did not unduly worry the watching crew of the *Diamond* as, provided Smith and his comrades had not been killed but merely captured, the custom for dealing with captured officers who gave their parole was not necessarily to imprison them but to allow to find their own accommodation until they could be exchanged for an officer of similar rank. Smith and Wright could therefore expect to be kept as prisoners for a few months until they could be exchanged for French prisoners held by the British.

However, there were some curious aspects of Smith's sortie which hinted that he had been engaged in a clandestine venture as well as a routine cutting-out exercise. It was highly unusual for the commander to take part in such an exercise—although his excuse was that some of his junior men were sick or unavailable—and more so for him to be accompanied by people such as Wright and Tromelin.

John Wesley Wright was twenty-six, which was old for a midshipman. He described his role on board ship as "the secretary of his friend". Earlier in his life, he had served as a volunteer in the Royal Navy. In 1780 he had taken part in the defence of Gibraltar. Returning to England, he spent two years at a school in Wandsworth before accepting employment in a City merchant's office, a post which took him to Russia, where he lived for five years and became fluent in the language. He was also proficient in French. How he met Smith is unknown, but Smith was impressed with his abilities and had encouraged him to resume his naval career as a midshipman until such time as he could take his lieutenant's examination. The naval role was a cover for more covert activities, which included spending lengthy periods in France, sometimes accompanied by Antoine Le Picard de Phélippeaux, a French royalist military engineer who had emigrated from France to England but who had returned in 1795 to resume his counter-revolutionary activities.

Tromelin was a twenty-five-year-old lieutenant in a royalist regiment who had survived the disaster at Quiberon Bay, south of Brittany, the previous year. This was a failed attempt by French counter-revolutionary forces to incite revolt in western France, bring an end to the revolution, and restore the monarchy. As an émigré captured on French soil, Tromelin knew that he would be executed were he to be recognised. He was therefore using the name of John Bromley and passing himself off as Smith's French-Canadian servant. He did not usually sail with Smith and was part of an intelligence network based in the Channel Islands which was run by Captain Philippe d'Auvergne.

For all three men to have run the risk of being captured in what was a routine naval operation seems extremely foolhardy unless, of course, an espionage mission was also involved. It is very feasible that Smith was returning from this mission when, chancing upon the *Vengeur*, he was unable to resist an attempt at capture, perhaps, according to one biographer, "wishing to give [Tromelin] the spectacle of a sensational feat of reckless sailing."

Smith was subjected to a long interrogation in Le Havre, after which he was immediately taken under a strong escort to Paris. Wright and

Tromelin, who had convinced the authorities that he was John Bromley, accompanied Smith to L'Abbaye de St Germain, a mediaeval monastic building that that been converted into a prison. The remaining crew had been marched off to Rouen.

Smith and Wright had been designated as state prisoners rather than as prisoners of war, which meant that neither could be exchanged for French officers in the accepted manner. This was ominous because the members of the Directory, which was the governing committee of the French First Republic, established in November 1795, were fully aware that Smith had been responsible for burning half the French fleet in Toulon. Their justification was that, because during that time Smith did not hold a commission and was not in uniform, he could be accused of incendiarism. But as he had acted under the orders of Lord Hood, there was little chance the charge would be sustained. Wright could not face the same charge as he was not present at Toulon, but a further accusation had been made against both men: that they had been attempting to burn the town and dockyard of Le Havre.

This charge was eventually formalised by an act of accusation signed by a member of the Directory, Paul-François Barras, but it was in effect a means of holding Smith and Wright outside the normal prisoner exchange system while the French sought information from which the men could be accused of espionage. If such information were to be found, it could easily result in Smith's death warrant.

On 3 July 1796, Smith, Wright, and Bromley were transferred from L'Abbaye to another prison, the Temple, which was used for housing condemned prisoners. It was an intimidating enough place to quail even the most hardened arrivals. Smith was told that he would be in solitary confinement but that his servant, John Bromley, would be permitted to visit him and attend to his needs.

The French were fully aware that Britain was helping the royalist espionage organisation Agence de Paris, and with the help of the Royal Navy, the British spymaster William Wickham could ferry royalist agents to and from France. With Smith and Wright both being fluent in French, and with Smith being on particularly friendly terms with French émigrés in England, it seemed highly likely that both men were counter-revolutionaries.

The capture of Smith and Wright was a source of embarrassment for the British government as both men were secret agents who were involved not only in espionage but also in royalist attempts to subvert the French government from within.

Nevertheless, the government, mainly in the form of Evan Nepean at the Admiralty, William Windham as secretary of war, and Grenville at the Foreign Office, made strenuous efforts to negotiate their release, only to be met with rebuffs. The Admiralty, though, took the initiative of sending a French officer, Jacques de Bergeret, captured in 1796 with the frigate *Virginie*, to Paris on parole with the expectation that Smith would be released in exchange. Both men were of equal rank, but the Directory was not interested and the officer was sent back.

Negotiations by the government continued throughout the remainder of 1796, with James Harris, Earl of Malmesbury, as leader of an unsuccessful delegation that went to Paris in October and well into 1797, when on 4 September the event known as the Coup of 18 Fructidor occurred. Several members of the Directory launched a coup d'état and seized control, purging the legislative body of its conservative members and placing Paris under martial law. The French approach then became more hostile, and discussions came to a halt. The British government felt that it had exhausted every recognised official avenue, yet Smith and Wright remained incarcerated in the Temple Prison.

Now the only realistic means of securing their release was through covert means. This where Richard, who had been living in France for much of 1796, could now take a much more decisive role.

The Escape from the Temple Prison

The Temple Prison

Within weeks of Smith and Wright's capture, the British government had begun to explore stealthier methods of securing their release in tandem with diplomatic methods. Their main channel was through Normandy royalists under the leadership of Louis Frotté, a group with whom Smith was also in contact at the time of his capture, but the group soon suffered defeat under General Lazare Hoche's mobile columns from the Vendée and Brittany. In June, Frotté fled to London, where he would remain until April 1797. He left behind him a large group of recalcitrant chevaliers whose options were now severely limited. One of these was Wright's companion Phélippeaux, who would soon play a major role in Smith's escape.

Although Smith and Wright had been placed in solitary confinement with Smith incarcerated in the rooms on the third floor of the central tower, once graced by Louis XVI before he was taken to be executed, communication did become possible between William Wickham and Smith, and money was supplied to the prisoners through these channels. Wickham also allocated a sum of £1,000 to royalist agents in Paris to assist in Smith's escape. The money certainly improved the two prisoners' daily existence, and since life under the Directory was largely driven by bribery and corruption, it also created opportunities for escape.

From his vantage point high up in his cell, Smith's hopes were lifted when he caught sight in the house opposite of the three mysterious royalist women who had first contacted him using a visual code during his time in L'Abbaye. He had nicknamed them the Three Muses, and now he was able to resume his signalling to them. Although they were unable to help the prisoners themselves, they too could arrange for money to be smuggled into the prison. Almost certainly by means of bribery, Smith was permitted to leave the gaol for a few hours at a time. Tromelin, who was still successfully maintaining his disguise as Smith's servant, had already been allowed to run errands for Smith. He had been able to meet up not only with supportive royalists but also with his wife, who proved to be a useful aid in the escape plans.

In January 1797, three royalist leaders who were part of the vital espionage network Agence de Paris were imprisoned in the Temple. Wickham wanted their immediate release. The Comte de Rochecotte, who commanded the royalist units to the west of Paris, was given the task of organising an escape. He selected three men to achieve this They were Phélippeaux; Boisgirard, who was a dancer at the Opéra; and Jean Hyde de Neuville, who had assumed a nom de guerre—L'Oiseau.

Smith and Wright were to be included in the escape plot, which involved digging a tunnel which ran from the prison's outer wall to the exercise yard. Unfortunately, the earthworks collapsed, but nobody was injured. On 1 February the responsibility for Smith's custody was transferred from the Department of Justice to the Ministry of Marine. And through Smith's persuasion, the minister, Georges-René Le Peley de Pléville, agreed to grant Tromelin his freedom. Tromelin was able to return to England in July.

Any further escape plans that might have been brewing were firmly dashed on 4 September following the Coup of 18 Fructidor. In its aftermath, two of the royalist prisoners were transported and the other was released, having turned informer. There was now little enthusiasm from L'Oiseau to devise a plan merely to help Smith and Wright.

At this point, the British Admiralty took decisive action by introducing Richard Cadman Etches into the arena. Having recently returned from his activities in France, he was back living in London, and he had written to Earl Spencer, First Lord of the Admiralty, offering his services.

Now that the responsibility for Smith and Wright came from the Ministry of Marine, Richard's connections with them made him an excellent choice to take over as leader of the escape group. Another recruit to the group was Count Antoine Marstin Viscovitch, who, like Richard was an experienced international agent but one who had a chequered past. He was a former officer in the Venetian navy and had been employed by the Alien Office, but now he was working for Paul Barras at the Directory and was deeply involved in bribery and money laundering by investing in *biens nationaux*, of which Barras was the main beneficiary. A recent transaction had become public knowledge, and Viscovitch had been thrown into the Temple himself for a short time as the escape plot was crystallising.

By December, Smith had become increasingly impatient over the interminable delays in securing his release. He continued to be allowed out for short periods, to dine either with Wright or with others at a small restaurant at the corner of the rue de La Loi and the rue St Honoré which was run by a Madame Séguin, an Irishwoman who was married to a Parisian.

Pléville was keeping an eye on Smith's activities. On 17 February 1798, following enquiries, he told the minister of police, Pierre Jean Sotin, that he had received evidence that Smith had formed an escape plan and would take flight within ten days. He was soon given details of a supper party that Smith had attended at Madame Séguin's restaurant on the night of 18 February.

Present at the party were John Alexander Keith, who was the nephew and assistant of William Herries, the manager of the Paris branch of a London bank named Herries, Farquhar, & Co.; Patrick Brennan, an Irish shipmaster; and a Mr Thompson, who was described as a "police agent who must be known at the Bureau Centrale". Keith's activities had apparently attracted the attention of the counter-espionage police, who had decided to position Thompson in the restaurant. He was an English teacher permitted to remain in Paris on the understanding that he would provide services as an informer. That evening he had been rewarded when he overheard a conversation in which a less than discreet Brennan declared that he had been asked to provide a vessel in which to take Smith back to England. No doubt Thompson was Pléville's informer.

Another man present was a Mr Driskett, an English subject said to have recently arrived from Baltimore. He never appears again under that name, and he left for Le Havre within a few hours of the supper party. According to author Elizabeth Sparrow, it is likely that Driskett was Richard Cadman Etches.

Patrick Brennan, who, besides being an Irish ship's captain of American ancestry, was a British agent, was questioned by police, but they left him free to leave for Boulogne. More likely it was Brennan who had arrived from Baltimore, not Richard.

Pléville requested information on all neutral vessels in the Channel ports, but he was too late. Both Driskett and Brennan had sailed. Although he was about to leave Paris to attend a meeting in Lille, Pléville found time to send an urgent warning to Sotin in which he demanded that one guard should be posted to watch Smith and that another be posted to make sure that Smith's gaoler did not grant him any more leaves of absence.

But this warning arrived too late because Smith was already making himself ready for his escape. The success of the plot to free him and Wright was dependent upon a piece of headed paper from the Ministry of Marine.

On the morning of 24 April, a fiacre, which is a four-wheeled cab, arrived at the door of the Tower of the Temple gates, and two officers, in the dress uniform of the National Guard, got out, leaving a third man inside and a fourth seated next to the driver.

The younger officer presented himself to Boniface, the prison governor, as Captain Armand Auger. In fact, his real name was Boisgirard. The older one gave his name as du Roy, but he was really one of Phélippeaux's officers named Le Grand de Palluau. He handed over an order written on Ministry of Marine letterhead, signed by Pléville, for the collection of Smith and Wright and for their transfer to a prison at Fontainebleau. Boniface passed the paper to the *greffier* (clerk) to inscribe the details in the prison register while he sent a turnkey to fetch the two men.

Smith was in no hurry to leave. He asked the concierge to line up the Temple staff, and he then presented each one with a gold louis while Auger signed for the prisoners. Smith and Wright walked out of the Temple as if they had been honoured guests of the Directory. Outside the gates, in the street, the fiacre was waiting. Glancing upwards, Smith saw that the man sitting next to the coachman was Tromelin, who had recently returned from England, having met with Pitt and Grenville to discuss Smith's escape. Inside, acting as footman, was Phélippeaux, who had organised the details of the escape plan and was now responsible for getting Smith and Wright to safety. Standing at the roadside were Hyde de Neuville, Viscovitch, and two more royalist agents who were ready to intervene in case of trouble.

The fiacre sped off, but in its haste, it struck a bollard, broke a wheel, and hit a small child. An angry crowd soon gathered. The occupants of the cab were forced to flee on foot and make their way to rue de l'Université, where they were able to spend the night in a safe house.

The following morning, Smith and Wright left with Phélippeaux on their journey to the coast, but as they had neither passports nor travel documents, they knew that the journey would be fraught with danger. The first obstacle would be the gates of Paris, where there would be barriers and guards to overcome. Phélippeaux had anticipated this by arranging their travel in a fresh carriage which had recently arrived from Nanterre. And he had a permit for the return journey. Just before the coach reached the gates of Paris, however, it hit a wall along the narrow streets and was slightly damaged. The occupants got out. While the guards were examining the coach and interrogating the driver, Smith and Wright managed to slip past them. They were able to rejoin the vehicle once it had been passed through the barrier.

As they continued their journey towards Rouen, they fully expected the sounds of pursuers, but none came. It had taken the authorities some time to discover that the transfer document presented at the Temple was a forgery and that Smith and Wright had not been taken to Fontainebleau. By the time the authorities had made this discovery and alerted the gates of Paris, the various checkpoints and had circulated descriptions of Smith and Wright, they were long gone, safe in the home of a royalist in Rouen while their passports were being forged.

Once in receipt of their passports, and now dressed in rough seamen's clothes, they made their way across the Seine to Honfleur, where a small fishing boat had been prepared for them. Soon they were at sea and on their way to safety.

In the English Channel, a frigate called *Argo* was sighted, and Smith and Wright were welcomed aboard by its captain, James Bowen. On 7

May, they were in sight of Portsmouth, and from there they made their way to London, where they arrived the next day.

The delight of the government was matched by joyful celebrations in the streets from a British public that had, during the past year, been on the receiving end of so much grim and disquieting news about the French and their many triumphs under Napoleon.

Firstly, Smith went to his mother's house, where he introduced Phélippeaux to her as the man who had rescued him. From here he reported to the Admiralty, who afterwards sent him to Whitehall to meet with the prime minister, William Pitt, and the Foreign Secretary, Lord Grenville. Smith's triumphant return was finalised with an audience with the king, George III.

Back in Paris on the next morning following the escape, Boniface reported to the minister in writing, including every detail of his orders. No questions were asked. But when a week later it was known that Smith and Wright were safely aboard a British frigate, the storm broke. Although he had only been following orders, Boniface was arrested and ended up being incarcerated in his own prison. Even though Pléville and Pierre Jean Sotin, Minister of Police, were only following orders as well, Paul Barras had them relieved of their ministerial posts.

Viscovitch and John Keith were also arrested, but Grenville gave orders that they must be allowed to escape. There is no record as to how this was achieved, but they were soon returned to England. Perhaps Barras was told that the final sum for his bribe may not have been available unless they were also set free.

But it was the Comte de Rochecotte who suffered the worst fate. Arrested by the Directory under the name of Rozette, he refused to provide information, even his proper name, and was taken before a military tribunal and shot. Upon hearing the news, Smith said insufficient gold had been available to save him from his fate.

The Involvement of Richard Cadman Etches

Until recently, it was believed that at the end of 1797, when their negotiator, James Harris, the 2nd Earl of Malmesbury, left France after his discussions had stalled, the British government had lost interest in securing

Smith's release. Tom Pocock, in his book *A Thirst for Glory*, writes, "The British government seemed to have abandoned attempts to negotiate his release." Another author, Peter Shankland, wrote, "The British government made no further effort to help him."

A perception has been created by several commentators that the escape was masterminded and organised by French royalist agents alone.

More recent research, mainly by Elizabeth Sparrow, has demonstrated that this is not the case. In her books *Secret Service: British Agents in France 1792–1813* and *Phantom of the Guillotine*, she has righted these wrongs and has credited Richard with the role he played in the escape of Sir Sidney. I have cross-referenced her account with Richard's memoirs to see how the two stories dovetail—or otherwise.

Part of the reason why Richard does not get a mention lies with Smith himself. He was known to be a loquacious and highly strung character. Dismissive of Smith's failure to burn every ship in Toulon harbour, Nelson once said of him, "Great talkers do the least we see." But upon his return to England, Smith was the soul of discretion, not only obfuscating the role of the British secret service in his escape but also accentuating the efforts of the royalists. He soon made Phélippeaux something of a hero by describing him as his daring rescuer.

Knowing that his father would broadcast the news of his escape to all and sundry, Smith would only give him a partial and distorted account of his escape: "The Directory having ordered a general assemblage of all English Prisoners together in One Prison, my Friends the royalists contrived to offer me the means of escape which by their assistance was effectuated most happily." He made no reference to Richard's role nor to that of any of the others who were working for the British secret service.

But this stance delighted the British government, who were anxious to hide the role played by their agents, not only for operational reasons but also because the lives of many of them remained at risk.

It was not until 20 May that Viscovitch was deported. By October, Keith had twice been imprisoned in the Temple on suspicion. Richard's agent in Rotterdam, Wilby, who had moved to Paris to look after his mercantile affairs, had also been arrested. Finally, Richard himself had been the subject of "a thundering denunciation", an "effectual outlawry" by Nicholas Madgett, the Irish-born official of the Green Cravat Gang. The gang comprised the United Irishmen in Paris who were plotting a French invasion of their country.

Fortunately, none of these agents was prosecuted, and Viscovitch and Keith, as well as several other royalists who were involved in the plot, went to the Mediterranean with Smith and Wright in 1799, fighting in Egypt and at the Siege of Acre.

Their escape may have been linked to bribery, but there is no doubt that silence from England helped to protect them, as did the government-financed press in London. Only when French newspapers revealed what had happened did it show that considerable planning had gone into the escape. But still no mention was made of the secret service involvement. Only the *Times* reported that "a Foreigner of some distinction" had undertaken a plan which had been formulated in England. But the outbreak of rebellion in Ireland in May 1798 soon diverted attention away from it.

Now let us look at Richard's memoirs insofar as they concern Smith's escape to see how they compare with what is now the accepted version of events and what they may add to that version. Bear in mind that even in his memoirs Richard may not have felt at liberty to reveal the whole story.

Richard states that at the time of Smith and Wright's incarceration, he was in Rotterdam. We know that he had mercantile interests in Holland and that he employed an agent, Wilby, whom he later moved to Paris to manage his affairs there. As his main residence was 19 Bryanston Street, London, he was presumably on a business trip and attending a public dinner there with a party of Americans. It was here that he learned from one of them, whose brother was also imprisoned in the Temple, that the monetary allowances to support Smith, Wright, and several other prisoners with whom they were friendly had been stopped. Aware of the distress that this would cause, Richard resolved to travel to Paris "for the purpose of serving Sir Sidney". As soon as he arrived, he obtained an order of fifty louis on a loan from the bank of Messrs Herries, Farquhar & Co. For some considerable time, this bank had been the conduit for channelling money for use in bribery and espionage. John Keith, who had worked there since 1793, was the nephew of William Herries. Keith also became Richard's right-hand man in the escape plot.

Richard states goes on to say that he immediately conveyed the money to Smith with a note secreted inside an orange. This note revealed Richard's identity to him and a plan by which he thought that Smith could escape. Sir Sidney replied that the wife of the concierge, that is the gaoler, would have to be bribed.

Accepting that bribery would have to play a major part in his plan, Richard sped off to London to discuss the option with Lord Spencer and other lords of the Admiralty. They highly approved of his proposal, but as previous attempts had failed, they "doubted the practicality" of his efforts. But Richard was confident that "money, properly made use of in Paris, would effect almost any undertaking." He returned to Paris and soon "got access to the Temple and the prisoners". He seemed to be able to enter and leave the Temple with the utmost ease.

Sparrow's book confirms that both Richard and Keith found the means to enter the Temple at will. Initially Richard might have achieved this by claiming to be a friend of the American prisoner, although he does not mention this in his memoirs. It was the custom for prisoners to have their meals sent to their own order and preference. The people who delivered meals were known as *traiteurs*. Perhaps Richard gained entry by posing as one. This would explain Sir Sidney's constraint and the reason why he only exchanged a few words with Richard at any one time.

But we also know that Smith and Wright were permitted to come out of the Temple at night, albeit sometimes accompanied by the gaoler. Richard claims that with the involvement and advice of Phélippeaux, he managed to set up several private meetings, at which the practicability of his plans was discussed.

Smith gave Richard a letter to be delivered to Lord Spencer. Once again, Richard sped off to London, fully confident that the necessary funds would be advanced to him because of the "very flattering manner" in which his project had been received by the Admiralty.

He was told that he should apply to the newly formed Transport Board for an advance of money to fund his project. Richard went ahead with the necessary application, but it was refused on the basis that every previous attempt to secure Smith's release had been unsuccessful. However, Evan Nepean told Richard that if he could raise the necessary funds himself and then Smith's release, the money that he had spent in the undertaking would be repaid to him by Lord Spencer.

Returning to Paris, Richard set about raising the funds. He says that he took John Keith, whom he describes as "cashier of the banking house of Messrs Herries & Co.", to meet Smith at one of their nightly meetings at the theatre. Keith, understandably, proved to be highly adept in the proper management of the funds.

In an undated communication to Evan Nepean, Richard had explained that having "advanced 13,000 livres and entered into an Engagement to previously deposit 35,000 plus 48,000 (together making 83,000) in the hands of Herries & Co.", he had not "heard of any difficulty whatever in completing that Engagement". Now, according to Elizabeth Sparrow, Richard expected Sir Sidney Smith to "return to England within fourteen days".

How was this money spent? There are two possibilities, and both could involve Viscovitch. Smith later told Nepean that he was "the person on whom the question depended". Does this imply that he used his influence at the Ministry of Marine to get hold of the headed paper signed by Pléville?

Viscovitch was also well connected to Paul-François Barras, the president of the Directory. Although responsibility for the prisoners' welfare rested upon Pléville with funds provided by Britain, it was to Paul Barras, the president of the Directory, not to Pléville, that on 16 January 1798 Herries had written:

> The funds are already at the disposition of the Minister of Marine and ready to be drawn upon, as I am assured, at the Trésorie Nationale

Herries's wording suggests that Pléville had not informed Barras that British money was in Paris ready for use. He may well have known also that the sum available was far more than was necessary for the "escape".

It seems likely that Barras had finally succumbed to the efforts to bribe him which had begun back in 1797. It is highly possible that Pléville took part in the bribe too. On the day that Herries had told Barras that British funds were available at the Trésorie Nationale, Pléville gave the order for the Directory's commissionaire for the Department of the Seine to collect all British prisoners, regardless of rank, and transport them all into one prison at Fontainebleau.

It is now impossible to untangle the various payments, bribes, and transactions that were involved in the escape plot, but from the record of Lord Spencer's disbursement of secret service funds, we can see that upon their return to England in 1798, Smith was reimbursed with £1,514 on 16 June, and further sums amounting to £376 were paid later in the year. Richard was given £1,200 in January and a further £900 in June.

Believing that the Mr Driskett who had attended the supper was Richard, Elizabeth Sparrow goes on to state that he was also likely to be the "Richard Cadman Etches who had been involved in the early stages of the bribe for Barras in 1797 and had been granted access to Sir Sidney Smith in prison".

But just as everything was ready, Richard was informed by the wife of one of the French government secretaries, who was in on the secret, that he had been denounced for having held certain communications with Smith. Although the denunciation that forced Richard to leave Paris was made by Nicholas Madgett of the Green Cravat Gang, his source was a Frenchman called Gadole who worked at the Ministry of Marine and who had watched Richard's every move as he visited the ministry and the Temple Prison.

Evan Nepean's correspondence from October 1798 says that Richard had warned him that a Frenchman named Gadole had been seen in London:

> [Previously] a principal commissaire in Belgium … I know him sufficiently to be confident that he will have Agents about all the Offices of Government more particularly the Marine from belonging to it in Paris.

Richard states that he left Paris the day after he was denounced. If he were indeed the Mr Driskett who attended the supper party on 18 February, he certainly left "within hours" of it and sailed off. He may not have been aware that Thompson was a French spy. There is mention of Mr Driskett having arrived from Baltimore, which seems highly improbable. As stated earlier Patrick Brennan, the American shipmaster, was more likely to have arrived from Baltimore rather than Richard.

Setting off in the morning without a single item of luggage, Richard says he arrived at Calais and instantly embarked for England. While his ship was pulling away from the pier, two French courtiers arrived from Paris with orders to arrest him. He says that the vessel almost certainly would have been ordered to return had it not been for a British cruiser that was anchored between his ship and the pier. He felt that had he been arrested, there was no doubt that he would have been "shot, without a judge or jury".

Upon his arrival in England, Richard communicated the arrangements he had made for Smith's release to Evan Nepean. Soon after this, he received a letter, in cipher, from John Keith which had been delivered to him via the dispatches of the French minister of marine to Mr Otto, who was the commissioner for French prisoners in London. Mr Otto had affixed his official seal to the letter and sent it to Richard by a trusted servant.

Mr Otto is almost certainly referring to Louis-Guillaume Otto, a Germano-French diplomat who was born in Baden in 1754. He studied at the University of Strasbourg and then entered the French diplomatic service. In 1779 he was dispatched to the newly formed United States of America on a diplomatic mission. Returning to France at the end of 1792, he was appointed the first head of the Political Division for Foreign Affairs, but the fall of the Girondins led to his dismissal and arrest. Close to being guillotined, Otto survived and went to Berlin. He was not posted to London as commissioner responsible for French prisoners of war until 1800, two years after Sir Sidney's release. Therefore, although Richard's memory may have been at fault here, it is almost certain that he would have known Otto.

Otto would come into public prominence on 1 October 1801 when Britain's prime minister, Henry Addington, accepted Napoleon's approach for peace. As the French emissary Otto, together with the foreign secretary, Lord Hawkesbury, signed the preliminary peace declaration which led to the Treaty of Amiens, ending the war with France. There were great celebrations in London and for days afterwards the streets were ablaze with brilliant displays. Everybody was expected to light up their houses with decorations. Naturally "Citizen" Otto's residence in Portman Square, close to Richard's home, was the *pièce de resistance*. An illuminated inscription announced: "Peace and Universal Happiness".

Richard took John Keith's letter to the Admiralty. At first sight, the contents of the letter seemed to be concerned with the provisions of various kinds of meat, but this was a form of code that was used to describe the fugitives. Richard deciphered the letter and confidently pronounced that Sir Sidney would arrive within twenty-four hours. This proved to be correct: Smith did arrive, and he dined the following day at Wimbledon.

In the evening of that day, while at Camelford House, which was the home of Thomas Pitt, the 2nd Baron Camelford (although he seldom lived there), Richard says he learned that Smith would be spending the night at the Prince of Wales Hotel, Conduit Street. On Monday morning he called at the hotel. The moment Sir Sidney saw him, he took Richard in his arms and, carrying him from one end of the coffee room to the other, placed him on a table. Embracing him affectionately, Sir Sidney exclaimed several times in the presence of the many gentlemen who were in the room, "Here is my Deliverer!" There is no reason to disbelieve that.

It would be safe to state that if Phélippeaux organised the escape plan and Viscovitch and Keith handled the financial side, then Richard Cadman Etches was the mastermind behind the whole operation.

The Anglo-Russian Invasion of Holland, August–November 1799

According to the memoirs, Richard returned to England from Holland in 1797 armed with information he had obtained about the naval and military strength of the country, as well as with "manuscript charts of the Zuider Zee, and of inland waters together with plans and drawings of the fortifications, the number and force of the shipping belonging to the States of Holland".

He then presented a plan to the Admiralty which set out not only an attack upon the island of Texel but also a plan for leading a naval force, accompanied by troops, from there through the inland waters to the Western Scheldt. It had always been thought that it would be impractical to make a successful attack on Amsterdam by this means, and therefore the idea had never been proposed despite Amsterdam having "adopted no means of defence".

But Richard was no "visionary schemer", and he never recommended a plan unless he was thoroughly convinced of its practical working. On this occasion, he had even ascertained the depth of the different waters and had assessed the rocks, the bridges, and the shoals from the entrance of the Texel to Flushing, and every other point that would be essential to the success of such an expedition. He wrote to Evan Nepean: "I know the beach well from having made a practice when at the Helder of bathing every morning … to convince myself. I am therefore confident that the troops might [be] landed from open Boats in safety."

In his secret correspondence with Evan Nepean, Richard had been urging action against Holland for some years. In June 1799, when the Second Coalition, negotiated by William Pitt and William Wyndham Grenville, was signed with Russia, Austria, and lesser powers, his hopes were lifted. The armies of the Second Coalition had been successful at pushing back the French in the early part of the year, and Pitt was keen to maintain the momentum by attacking the outlying parts of their "empire".

In August, Britain and Russia decided to launch an invasion of the Batavian Republic in the northern part of Holland. The objectives were to neutralise the Batavian naval fleet and to instigate an uprising to bring down the French-controlled Batavian government.

The British land forces were assembled near Canterbury, Kent, under the command of Lieutenant General Sir Ralph Abercromby. The question arose as to the best place to make an amphibious landing. Several locations along the Dutch coast were considered, but eventually the area south of Den Helder, as suggested by Richard, was chosen as the landing place.

The invasion met with early success. The depleted Dutch fleet under Rear Admiral Samuel Story evaded conflict, thus permitting British troops to disembark unopposed near the town of Callantsoog, where Abercromby won a convincing victory against the Batavian army. When Story belatedly decided to engage the British fleet, he found that he had a fullyfledged mutiny on his hands. This led to the Vlieter incident on 30 August where his whole fleet with 632 guns and 3,700 men surrendered to Admiral Andrew Mitchell.

As a result of the surrender, the British fleet had taken control of not just the North Sea but also the Zuider Zee, but they did not seize the advantage of this by making an amphibious landing at Amsterdam, which, for a few days, lay totally defenceless against an attack. If they had, the campaign may possibly have ended there and then. One can only imagine Richard's emotions on learning this.

In his memoirs, Richard states that his plan was accepted by the Admiralty, and it was decided that an expedition under the command of Abercromby and Mitchell aboard HMS *Isis* would be undertaken. Richard accompanied them as a volunteer and had the satisfaction of seeing that the two men were using his identical plans, charts, and drawings for the guidance of the expedition.

On arrival off the Dutch coast, the only doubt that Mitchell had was whether they could find pilots who were familiar with the Texel passages, but Richard reassured him that as soon as the sandhills of the Helder Peninsula had been overcome, Texel pilots could be procured, and they would steer the fleets safely in.

Richard says that he was present at the "attack on the sandhills". This must refer to what became known as the Battle of Callantsoog, when Abercromby's troops disembarked unopposed and later defeated the Dutch army. He also claims that the following morning he had accompanied Mitchell into the Texel and witnessed the surrender of Admiral Story. Every ship that he saw had been recorded on his list. The number was forty-four.

The territorial campaign was far from being over, though. Richard says that he volunteered his services for the forthcoming battles and was present for every one of them. His role is not explained, but in one engagement he received a severe wound. Richard gives no more detail, but the injury may well have occurred at the Battle of Alkmaar on 2 October 1799. This was a hard-fought engagement in which French sharpshooters killed and wounded several British soldiers, mainly officers.

Following the retreat from Alkmaar, and before Abercromby re-embarked at Texel, he sent for Richard and asked him whether he had preserved his "red book". This book was a diary containing all the information that Richard had passed onto the general and the admiral, as well as the observations he had made during the campaign.

Upon hearing that the book was still in Richard's possession, the general said that he would give him a letter setting out the importance of his services and that he should present it to Lord Spencer. Admiral Mitchell gave Richard a similar letter to present to Lord Spencer.

Unfortunately, the capture of the Dutch fleet had little impact on the war. The intelligence estimates of the extent of support that would come from the Dutch population were overly optimistic. Perhaps his field agents at the Texel and other ports had told him what he wanted to hear rather than the reality of the situation. However, it was in consequence of Richard's suggestions and comments that so many successful attacks were made on Dutch shipping within the Vlie (the tidal trench between Texel and the mainland), as well as within the islands situated north of Texel.

When Richard returned to London, he presented the two letters to Evan Nepean and confirmed to him that he was still in possession of his red book.

Richard was then told that under orders from His Majesty's minister, he should now retire to the country and write his own opinions regarding all the operations of the expedition. He was told not to conceal his feelings about the conduct of anyone who was involved and that he need not fear their displeasure because his observations were intended for the inspection of "the highest authority in the empire".

Richard obeyed the order and wrote a narrative of the expedition which extended to seventy pages. Unfortunately, not one word of this narrative has ever been made available to the public. I have no idea if it still exists or, if it does, where it could be. Perhaps it is lying in some musty-smelling box in a basement at the Admiralty.

The Battle of Copenhagen, 1801

The Battle of Copenhagen is mentioned in Dawson and Hobson's book as follows:

> On the fitting out of the expedition which had for its object the Danish fleet in the Copenhagen-roads, Mr. Etches transmitted to the British Admirals [Nelson and Parker] some valuable information relative to the state of the fortifications, and the naval preparations of the Danes.

As a neutral country, Denmark was in dispute with Britain over the British right to search Danish ships. Denmark claimed the right to trade with any country and to transport any goods, except for a narrow range of specific war materials. They felt that their ships should not be searched by the Royal Navy, and they would ignore any blockade treaties unless warships prevented them from entering a port.

From Britain's standpoint, if neutral vessels were not going to be searched, then they could break the British blockade of enemy ports at will. Britain therefore wanted a wider definition of the goods forbidden to be carried by neutral ships and, crucially, the power to search ships to enforce blockades. This was a matter of stopping French expansion and ultimately a matter of the very survival of the British Isles. For Denmark it meant money, as neutral ships were very much in demand. Many cargoes supposedly destined for Denmark were instead being transported to France and its allies. Ships of other nations were also sailing under the Danish flag as cover.

Following Nelson's victory in Egypt, the Mediterranean was now under the control of the Royal Navy, who were trying to blockade French and Spanish ports. Britain maintained the right to search Danish ships while Denmark denied them that right. British warships were taking a closer look at Danish vessels.

Denmark's answer was to enter an alliance with other neutral nations to actively protect their ships from being stopped. It was known as the League of Armed Neutrality, which, at Denmark's prompting, was led by Russia. Denmark was playing a dangerous game because not only was Tsar Paul of Russia insane, but also his actions were unpredictable. Denmark had a stark choice: either to surrender to British pressure or to throw their lot in with the tsar. Gambling that Britain would take no action, they joined Russia, Sweden, and Prussia and hoped that with their support they might be able to negotiate a free trade deal with Britain for Danish ships. But within weeks of receiving Denmark's invitation to head the league, Tsar Paul had made secret overtures to Napoleon.

Denmark was now in a weak position. If war were to break out between Britain and Russia, Denmark would have to take Russia's side. The treaty was formed on 16 December 1800. Tsar Paul placed an embargo on all British ships in Russian ports and arrested all British citizens. This was the herald to a Franco-Russian alliance to dominate the continent with Denmark and Sweden as buffer states. The league members were now, in effect, Britain's enemies, and it was no longer merely a matter of preventing British ships from being searched. Now access to the Baltic States, which provided Britain with essential supplies such as timber and hemp, could be thwarted. Despite being fully aware that their country would be Britain's first target, Denmark snubbed all diplomatic approaches from them. In their minds, defiance of Britain was nowhere near as catastrophic for them as an invasion from Russia.

On the day that Nelson arrived back in Plymouth, the British government acted by detaining all Danish and Swedish ships in British ports and giving orders that any that were found at sea were to be captured. Although Russia was Britain's main aggressor, its bases at Kronstadt and Reval (now Tallinn) were situated farther north and would still be ice-bound when the thaw unlocked the Danish ports. Therefore, Copenhagen would be the first target.

The Admiralty chose Admiral Sir Hyde Parker to head the mission. Aged sixty-one, he had enjoyed a respectable, rather than a distinguished, naval career, much of it spent in the West Indies where he had become immensely rich from his share of the prize money obtained from the capture of foreign privateers. He was regarded as being politically sound and had been selected for his ability to conduct diplomacy. His orders were to prise Denmark away from the league either by "amicable arrangement or by actual hostilities". Then he was to launch "an immediate and vigorous attack" on the Russians at Reval and then Kronstadt.

Nelson, who was well known to the Danes, was to be his second-in-command. His job was to apply the iron fist should diplomacy fail. In theory, this was an ideal pairing of commanders, but the partnership was doomed to failure from the very beginning. Nelson, conscious of the need for urgency, was impatient for his flagship to be repaired and anxious to depart so that the Danish and Swedish fleets could be neutralised before Russia could come to their aid. Parker, though, was a naturally cautious person who moved slowly and was not prone to making instant decisions. This led to constant and unnecessary delays.

On 7 March, Nelson, his ships now in good order, sailed to Great Yarmouth to link up with Parker. Immediate friction arose between the two men over Parker's procrastination. Under pressure from Nelson, the fleet finally set sail on 12 March.

In December 1800, a hydrographer called John Mitchell, who had been supplying intelligence since 1796, gave an updated account of the Danish and Swedish fleets, adding that both governments would prefer to join Britain against Russia. He quoted the Prince Royal of Denmark as saying that "only a British fleet at the gates of Kronstadt could be a check on the power and pretensions of Russia". Mitchell supported this view. Richard had also recommended that the British attack take place at the port of Saint Petersburg rather than Copenhagen.

In the words of the author Dudley Pope, "The two British agents with the greatest knowledge of the Baltic and North Sea ports were both recommending attacking the Russian rather than the Danish Navy." However, this strategy would not be without its risks as it would leave the Danes and the ambivalent Swedes in control of the Sound—the route the British fleet would have to take on its return from Kronstadt.

On 19 March, the fleet reached the Skaw (Skagen) at the tip of Denmark, where they were joined by the three British diplomats whose brief had been to try to extricate Denmark from the league by "amicable arrangement". Parker had readied his ship for action but was awaiting feedback from the diplomats. One of them, Nicholas Vansittart, informed him and Nelson that the mission had failed to negotiate a last-minute settlement and that the only option now was war with Denmark, which had been preparing enormous defensive positions, helped by Parker's delay in sailing.

Vansittart later joined Parker and Nelson for a private discussion about the suggestion made by both Mitchell and Richard of using the Great Belt as an alternative to the passage in the Sound. Nelson wanted to attack the Danes immediately, but agreement was difficult, not only because of Parker's natural reticence but, according to one theory which has not found wide support, because through Britain's secret service, he would have known that plots were afoot for the assassination of both Napoleon and Tsar Paul. The death of the tsar would certainly change the situation and avert the need for war. But, as he was not free to reveal whether an assassination was imminent, Parker employed delaying tactics for eight days, despite having arrived in the Sound on 25 March. Finally, with no news coming from Saint Petersburg, he could stall no longer.

Copenhagen was a small city extending across a channel which separated the large island of Zeeland from a much smaller one named Amager. Because at their highest point the city walls sat barely twenty feet above sea level, the fortifications were not high enough to prevent bombardment from the sea. To counteract this, the Danes had anchored a motley line of barges, hulks, and warships along the edge of the channel to the north-east of the city to prevent the British from closing in on the land. To the north of this line, at the tip of a shoal, stood the Trekroner fort. The harbour entrance was further protected by another line of ships and hulks. Most of the ships were not fitted out for service at sea, but like the hulks, they were powerfully armed and had been turned into floating batteries which could be resupplied using gunboats, which were agile and could move speedily through the shallows.

The British view was that while the floating batteries were strong, the weakness would lie with the inexperience of the crews within them. The main concern was the shallow waters and treacherous shoals in the Sound.

Both Parker and Nelson had been briefed by men who had served in the Russian Navy, as well as by Mitchell and Richard, who had supplied them with hydrographic information and charts. Nelson was warned that the shallowness of the water south of Copenhagen would necessitate ships in the line having to decrease their draught by unloading their guns in order to get through the Sound into the Baltic, which is exactly what Nelson's ships had to do.

On the night of 31 March, the British fleet had anchored some seven miles north of Copenhagen, at a spot which was within sight of the city but well out of enemy range. A plan of attack was finally formulated: the fleet would split into two with Nelson, aboard HMS *Elephant*, taking his ships south and keeping to the east of the Middle Ground sandbank, while Parker would remain to the north-east of the battle to provide support and guard against ships coming from that direction. Parker had given Nelson the twelve ships of the line with the shallowest draughts and all the smaller ships in the fleet. It was imperative that while defeating the Danes, the British should lose the minimum of ships so that afterwards they could go on to attack the Russian fleet.

Although Nelson had been given much hydrographic advice from varying sources, he still had some concern about locating the deepest part of the channel. And for most of the night of 31 March, Captain Thomas Hardy was busy taking soundings up to the Danish line. Nevertheless, the British ships were not able to accurately locate the deepest part of the channel, so they were obliged to steer too far seaward.

Once the winds were favourable, Nelson would sail to the west of the sandbank and proceed northward to attack Copenhagen. He had reconnoitred the Danish fixed batteries' defences the previous day and found them to be exceptionally strong, so he knew that if he were to bring his whole fleet into immediate action, it would be outgunned. So, he decided that as his fleet approached the southern end of the Danish defences, his foremost ship would draw alongside a Danish ship, weigh anchor, and engage it. The rest of the line would pass outside the engagement until the next ship could draw alongside the next Danish ship and so on.

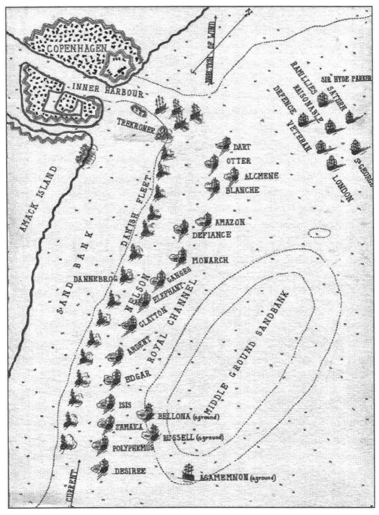

Battle of Copenhagen chart

Once the enemy ships had been subdued, troops would land and make an assault on the Trekroner fortress. Edward Riou, the captain of HMS *Amazon*, had been given the job of attacking the northern end of the enemy line. Should his forces be unable to subdue these stronger defences, once the Southern Fleet had been destroyed, bomb ships would be able to approach within range of the city and force negotiations to prevent its bombardment.

The next morning, 2 April, a favourable wind allowed Nelson's ships to steer around the Middle Ground sandbank, avoiding the Refshale shoal, but as neither was visible, his pilots could not agree upon the best course to aim for. Eventually, a pilot volunteered to guide the lead ship *Edgar* up the channel to Copenhagen. The other ships began to follow in their prescribed order, but the fifth, *Agamemnon*, ran aground on the Middle Ground sandbank, which ruined Nelson's precise sailing order. He was now forced to improvise. Then the sailing order was further disrupted when both *Bellona* and *Russell* ran aground. It now took Nelson even longer to reorganise his line to maximise his firepower. The wind was directly against Parker's ships, and it became obvious that it would take them a long time to reach the battle arena. They had to remain on standby, outside the impending fray, which began at 10.05 a.m.

By lunchtime, the battle was in full swing with both sides delivering broadsides, but as the day wore on, some of the Danish batteries ceased firing and some surrendered. Having made no further progress against the powerful headwind, Parker's ships had played no part in the battle. Because of the smoke from the guns, Parker was unable to see very much of the action, but he was aware of the three ships that had run aground, because two of them were flying distress signals.

Around 1.00 p.m. Parker issued a signal to "Discontinue the action". There has been some confusion as to why the signal the signal was sent. It may have been in the belief that Nelson had fought to a standstill but, without fresh orders, was unable to retreat. Of Nelson, Parker said, "If he is in a condition to continue the action, he will disregard it; if he is not, it will be an excuse for his retreat and no blame can be imputed to him." Shortly before the signal was made, Robert Otway, the captain of Parker's flagship was attempting to reach Nelson in a small craft. The reason has never been satisfactorily explained and it has led to theories that while the battle was raging Parker had somehow received news of the assassination of Tsar Paul in Saint Petersburg nine days earlier. He had therefore sent Otway, one of his closest and most trusted friends, to tell Nelson. The more likely scenario is that Otway had been sent to tell Nelson to cease action, but seeing his slow progress towards the *Elephant*, Parker panicked and issued the signal.

Nelson acknowledged the signal, but turning to his flag captain, Thomas Foley, he said, "You know, Foley, I only have one eye. I have a right to be blind sometimes." Then, holding his spyglass to his blind eye, he added, "I really do not see the signal." This was the origin of the expression "to turn a blind eye", but some people believe that this story about Nelson is apocryphal. The signal was repeated, but from a place which was invisible to much of the fleet. Ironically, Edward Riou was the only captain who did see the signal. Deciding that he must obey, he withdrew his forces, which were attacking the Trekroner fort as planned. Within minutes he was killed by a cannonball.

Although the Danes were fighting doggedly, it became obvious that they were sustaining increasing damage from Britain's superior gun power. Gradually the fixed batteries began to fall silent. With Otway having finally reached the *Elephant*, Nelson decided to call for a truce. A volunteer who spoke Danish, Captain Frederick Thesiger, was sent to deliver a letter from him to see Crown Prince Frederick, who had been watching the battle from the ramparts of the citadel. Nelson's note said that he had orders to spare Denmark provided it was no longer resisting, but if fighting continued, then he would be obliged to set fire to the floating batteries which he had captured.

The truce was agreed, and all action ceased. In reply to a response from the crown prince, Nelson wrote that the reason for his offering the truce was "humanity", adding that he would consider this "his greatest victory he has ever gained, if it may be the cause of a happy reconciliation between his own most gracious Sovereign, and his Majesty King of Denmark".

After the fighting had ended at 4 p.m., the Danish flagship, *Dannebrog*, exploded, killing 250 men. Estimates of Danish losses vary from between 1,135 and 2,215 captured, killed, or wounded. Of the Danish ships, two had sunk, one had exploded, and twelve had been captured. British casualties were 963 killed and wounded.

Nelson wrote his report of the battle and took it to Parker the following day. Parker had been given some simple instructions about the position he should adopt after the battle, but now aware of some complications that might ensue, he decided that his vice admiral would be a better negotiator. The following day, Nelson landed in Copenhagen to begin negotiations with the Crown Prince, in which he was able to secure an indefinite armistice. On 8 April, he also managed to obtain a formal agreement for Britain to protect Denmark.

After the battle, Nelson said:

> The Danes were the brothers of the Englishmen: there was no feud between England and Denmark to warrant the most desperate, the most bloody, the most frightful slaughter of each other!

The official news of Tsar Paul's death did not reach London until 13 April. The British fleet, which had moved on to attack the Russian ports in the Baltic, was recalled. On 5 May, Parker was also recalled and told to hand over his command to Nelson, who had sailed eastward. On finding out that negotiations had begun to end the Armed Neutrality agreement, he withdrew on 17 May.

It is hard to believe that as the British fleet departed from the Sound, more vessels ran aground. The fleet had been given advice charts and surveys by Richard, John Mitchell, and men who had served in the Russian Navy who must have sailed up and down the Sound on numerous occasions. Therefore, it is difficult to believe that the advice was faulty. Was it the fault of the Royal Navy's seamanship, or were the treacherous shoals and sandbanks to blame?

Raid on Boulogne, 2–3 October 1804

Since coming to power, Napoleon had made no secret of his desire to invade Britain. And this was a terrifying prospect. The French ports across the Channel provided an easy passage to British shores and represented the strongest threat. Preparations for an invasion flotilla had been ongoing since the late 1790s, but the Peace of Amiens, signed on 27 March 1802, had briefly ended hostilities. For several years, these ports had been closely watched. Activities inside them were monitored by people like Richard who had the ability to flit in and out of France without raising suspicion. Eventually the Royal Navy had set up a system of blockading the ports.

But by the turn of the century, matters had begun to escalate. Napoleon had begun to move more troops into large military camps and had situated landing craft around the strongly fortified ports of Boulogne and Calais. Several assaults had been made on the port of Boulogne, including one by Nelson in 1801, but because of its heavy fortification, they had been unsuccessful.

In 1803 a flotilla designed for the invasion of England began to assemble at Boulogne. Napoleon was there to watch its progress. His plan was to amass about two thousand boats to carry his Armée d'Angleterre across the Channel. Aware that the Royal Navy stood firmly in his way, he boasted that it was "necessary for France to be masters of the sea for six hours only, and England will have ceased to exist".

Things got worse for Britain in December 1804 when Spain declared war on Britain. This would now make it easier for the French fleet to break out of not only their main base at Toulon but also the Mediterranean itself.

Napoleon's troops were better organised and more experienced than the British Army who, despite their patriotism, would not be a match for the French. Nor were Britain's coastlines adequately fortified. Plans to strengthen them would not be put in place until the autumn of 1804, and it would take years before their completion. It was doubtful if Britain's land-based forces would withstand a French invasion in the south of the country and an onwards advance to London. Therefore the "wooden walls" of the Royal Navy would be the only way of protecting Britain.

The blockading of the French ports had allowed Britain some breathing space, during which the government prepared more ships for the sea and took steps to prevent the French from gaining control of the Channel, including the harassment of their ships as they gathered at the port of Boulogne.

But it was clear that other means of preventing a French invasion had to be considered. Prime Minister William Pitt began to meet with inventors and amateur tacticians who proposed innovative methods of attacking the French ships before they could put to sea. These ideas included releasing rocket-carrying balloons over the port at night to be detonated by clockwork, sending in a fleet of fireships or sinking blockships in the harbour mouth.

According to Dawson and Hobson, in 1804 Richard was asked by the Secretary of State to give his opinion on a proposal which had been submitted to the British government "for ruining the navigation of the harbour of Boulogne, and for dispersing the immense flotilla which Buonaparte had there assembled, for the invasion of Great Britain." Richard did not seem to be too impressed with the proposal as he promptly asked whether he could submit one of his own. He was immediately requested to do so.

His idea was to "equip three large vessels, of small draught of water, and to erect them on a solid body of masonry, united with cement, and so clamped with iron plates, screws, collars &c as to withstand the ebb of many tides: they were to be rigged as fire-ships, with a heavy tonnage of floating fire-works on board of each."

Richard was then asked that if his plan were to be adopted, would he be willing to "superintent its execution". He answered that he had "never submitted a project for which he had not volunteered his services to carry into effect". He was then ordered to appear before the Admiralty the following morning with an estimate of the probable cost of the undertaking. He did so. In February 1804, his plan was approved, and the sum of £10,000 was placed to his credit at the banking house of Hammersley & Co. in London.

Richard's memoirs do not provide any more detail about his plan, no doubt for a good reason, as we will see later. Fortunately, author James Earle, in his book about the rocket inventor Commodore Squib does provide more detail.

Richard had teamed up with an American merchant skipper called Captain Mumford. Their plan was to block the mouth of Boulogne harbour by using three ships filled with huge amounts of Portland stone and all the inflammatory material they could carry. Disguised as timber carriers and sailing under Dutch or Norwegian colours, they would pretend to be fleeing from the pursuit of British vessels and seeking refuge in Boulogne harbour. Upon arrival at a crucial spot in the approaches to the harbour, the ships would be set alight and would sink, becoming embedded in the sand and mud and thereby blocking the harbour entrance. The crews would escape by transferring swiftly to a cutter which, to further confound the enemy, would be flying French colours.

Richard's approach by the Secretary of State seems to have been prompted by the remarks of the First Sea Lord, the Earl of St Vincent, who in the final months of his tenure was asked about Richard. Rather distractedly, he described him as "a very intelligent man … much employed by the government". On this rather tenuous recommendation, Richard was approached for his opinion.

Now given the go-ahead, Richard purchased three rather old, decaying vessels which bore the names *Martha*, *Sally*, and *Betsy*. Soon, though, it became clear that the Portland stone could not be deposited in its loose form as it would quickly be washed away by the complex tides around Boulogne harbour. His plan had to be adjusted to enable "piers" to be constructed within each vessel so that the stone could be packed tightly within them and held together with iron bars and lead. Richard maintained that he could create stone masses nearly forty feet long, ten feet high, and seventeen feet wide. However, he felt that the work had to be carried out in great secrecy and with minimal accountability.

The Bank of England was under reconstruction at this time, and the governor assigned some of the stonemasons to Richard as a means of creating a plausible cover story. Rumours soon started that the huge amounts of stone were being made ready as foundations for houses that were going to be built on the shoal sands of Carolina. Unfortunately, nobody believed that story for one moment. By the time that Richard and Captain Mumford reached the Downs—an anchorage off Deal, Kent, which is inside the Goodwin Sands and sheltered from westerly winds—a week later, somewhat worse for wear after a collision at sea, the whole project had become a source of gossip.

The *Morning Herald* of 6 March 1804 had published a detailed report of what appeared to be going on. Admiral Lord Keith, who had been put in charge of the project, angrily described the three vessels as being "in a disgraceful state, with rotten ropes and sails, not worth £500 apiece".

Captain Mumford, whose navigational capabilities seemed to be seriously lacking, was dismissed by Keith as "an American", "not much of a seaman", and "wildly boastful". Richard was regarded as a drunkard who, with Mumford, had "projected nothing but to put money in their

[Richard and Mumford's] pockets and [then left] us to execute an ill-concerted plan".

Concluding that "these two men are not equal to such undertakings", Lord Keith had little alternative but to increase the level of naval assistance to fifty ratings (sailors)—a number that he could ill afford to lose. The Admiralty was complaining that, to prevent many of its vessels from lying idle, an additional twenty thousand men were needed. Now precious manpower was being diverted to ill-judged schemes instigated by incompetents.

Meanwhile, the detailed accounts about the expedition's progress published each day by the *Morning Herald* were probably providing the French with almost as much information as the Admiralty was receiving!

On 12 April 1804, the "stone ships" finally appeared off Boulogne with an embarrassed naval escort. The French responded immediately by mooring an additional defensive line of one hundred and fifty vessels outside the harbour. Rumour had it that the French actively wanted to assist the project so that the stone could be used to form the foundation for further fortifications. Were this so, then France would have received the poor end of the bargain.

Back in London, it was revealed that Richard's accounts had been shown to be "a little loose" and that the masonry had been neither properly fixed together nor inspected. *Martha*, *Sally*, and *Betsy* were recalled to Sheerness, and from there they arrived in the Thames. It was estimated that the "stone ships project" had cost the public purse something in the region of £16,000. St Vincent had already become unpopular because of his detailed investigation into corruption within the Royal Navy and his proposed reforms. He had made enemies of William Pitt and many influential men who were involved in moneymaking schemes. Now, to his fury, his opponents would use this debacle as part of the concerted attack against him and his life's work. He resigned as First Lord on 14 May 1804, just after William Pitt replaced Henry Addington as prime minister.

The Dawson and Hobson account of Richard's venture understandably glosses over the foregoing details. Its narrative ends with the following:

> The project, however, was eventually given up by the
> government, although there was little reason to doubt

but that it would have been successfully executed. It was admitted that Mr Etches had done his duty, and he was completely exonerated from all responsibility in the affair.

During the period from 30 January to 2 June 1804, Richard wrote around thirty letters about the blockade of Boulogne harbour. They were addressed to John Sullivan of Downing Street; Lord Melville; and Sir A. S. Hammond, Bart., at the Admiralty. These letters are now kept in the National Archives, Kew. The letters are brief and mostly concern the construction of stone ships. As an example, one letter encloses "a plan and two elevations of a stone pier to be built on board the ships *Daniel* and *De Meux*".

I am not aware that any of Richard's ideas were taken up, but he was not alone in proposing innovative methods of warfare which did not turn out to be successful. On 20 July 1804, William Pitt and Sir Home Popham met with the US-born inventor Robert Fulton, who had been working in France designing submarines but had received little interest from the French navy. He therefore came to Britain and offered his services to the Admiralty, proposing an assault on Boulogne harbour using a combination of fireships, torpedoes, mines, and other explosive devices. Pitt was persuaded, and Fulton was contracted to work with the Admiralty to construct his devices in anticipation of launching an assault later in the year.

Working at Portsmouth Dockyard, Fulton declared his inventions ready. An assault was planned for early October. He had built several types of craft and explosive devices, including a "torpedo catamaran" steered by a man with a paddle whose task was to approach a French ship, hook the torpedo onto the anchor cable, activate it by removing a pin, and then escape before it detonated. Fulton had also devised large numbers of casks filled with gunpowder, ballast, and combustible balls which were intended to float in on the tide and explode when washing up against the hulls of the enemy vessels. Finally, there were several fireships carrying forty barrels of gunpowder rigged to explode by a clockwork mechanism.

The British naval force had assembled outside Boulogne in late September, under the overall command of Admiral Lord Keith, aboard his flagship HMS *Monarch*. With him to witness the operation were Lord

Melville and Fulton himself. However, Keith had made no attempts to conceal the British force, so the French were soon alerted of the imminence of an attack. By 9 p.m. on the night of 2 October, conditions were judged as favourable and the flotilla approached the harbour in three divisions.

The French, having perceived the British threat, had reacted by anchoring their line of frigates farther inshore and deploying a protective line of pinnaces. These were light boats which were used as tenders to bigger craft. As soon as they spotted the approaching ships, the French sentries opened fire, depriving the men aboard the fireships the element of surprise. But steering full speed ahead, the British set the mechanisms and abandoned ship. The results were spectacular, but they achieved little: one fireship exploded in the gap between two frigates; another passed through the French line and exploded beyond it; and another was stopped by a pinnace. When the French crew boarded the pinnace and began a search, it blew up, killing those aboard. It also destroyed another pinnace alongside. This proved to be the only success of the night as the eighteen torpedo catamarans and the exploding casks proved to be ineffective. The British remained in action, however, until 4 a.m., when a gale forced them to seek shelter in the Downs.

The venture had turned out be a disappointing failure for the British. Fulton, claiming that his devices had not been deployed correctly, began to refine them. Despite being sceptical from the beginning, Keith was surprisingly sympathetic, declaring that his forces had been unlucky and that he thought another attempt might bring more success. Melville had similar views but added that the attack had no doubt spread panic among the French, who later began to construct a series of booms and chains across the harbour entrance to thwart any future attacks. With winter approaching, any plans for another attack would have to wait at least until the spring of 1805.

However, on 29 March 1805, the French fleet under Admiral Villeneuve did eventually manage to break out from the British blockades of its base in Toulon. If the fleet in Brest could also break out, the plan was to sail out of the Mediterranean, cross the Atlantic, and rendezvous at Martinique, giving the impression that they would be attempting to attack the West Indies. Nelson would be lured into pursuit, and while he searched for them, the fleets would double back, take control of the English Channel, and help transport the Armée d'Angleterre across to Dover.

It was also believed that French troops would also be landed in Ireland, where they would foment rebellion, but on 11 August 1804, in a secret report to the War Office, Richard apparently informed the British government that Napoleon had ordered an invasion of Ireland to coincide with that of England. Napoleon had clung onto this plan until October, by which time he had discovered that it had been irredeemably compromised and would have to be abandoned. After his debacle over the stone ships, perhaps Richard had redeemed himself.

Villeneuve was joined at Cadiz by six Spanish ships. The combined fleet reached Martinique on 12 May. They waited for the Brest fleet, but Admiral Ganteaume had found it impossible to breach the blockade and was unable to make the rendezvous. On learning that Nelson had arrived in Antigua, Villeneuve made his way back to Europe. On 22 July, as the Franco-Spanish fleet approached Cape Finisterre, it was met by a British fleet commanded by Admiral Robert Calder. Poor light and thick fog helped in creating confusion. The battle that followed proved to be indecisive even though both sides claimed victory. Villeneuve, licking his wounds, decided to make for Cadiz, much to Napoleon's fury. Now having to abandon his plans for the invasion of Britain, on 27 August Napoleon marched his army eastward to deal with the Austrian and Russian threat. Villeneuve and the combined fleets stayed in Cadiz until 21 October, when they emerged to be destroyed by Nelson at the Battle of Trafalgar. Sadly, Nelson was mortally wounded and died the same day.

Sir Sidney Smith—Aftermath

Although I can find no evidence that Richard and Smith ever worked together after Smith's release from the Temple Prison, in their own ways they continued to fight against the threat of Napoleon. Both were secret service agents, but whereas Richard carried on in a secret, clandestine way, Smith, who was also in the Royal Navy, enjoyed a career almost on the scale of Lord Nelson, although he did not receive as much public acclaim. Both men involved themselves in the attack on Boulogne, though.

Following his escape, Smith reached London on Tuesday, 8 May 1798.

Having visited Lord Spencer, the First Lord of the Admiralty, and having been received by King George, it was not long before his thoughts turned again towards the sea. He was desperate to return to action, and soon he was given the opportunity to do so. In a highly unusual move, he was offered a dual mission in which he would act as both a naval officer and a diplomat. It was a mission that would bring him into conflict with Lord St Vincent and Admiral Nelson, as well as lead up to the greatest triumph of his career: the defence of Acre.

By 1797, Napoleon's Grande Armée not only posed the serious threat of a British invasion but also had now placed the whole of the Mediterranean Sea at risk by taking undisputed control of the area. He had been building up his fleet at Toulon, and it was thought prudent for Britain to send a squadron of warships there. Its mission would be both one of armed reconnaissance and the prevention of the fleet from finding its way into the eastern Mediterranean. Smith was recommended to be appointed commander because he was known to the Turks and Russians. And following his escape from Paris, his fame as a national hero would be good for morale. He would be placed under the command of Lord St Vincent. Others thought that Nelson might be the better choice and it was he who was given command.

By the time Nelson reached Toulon, the armada had sailed. Nobody was sure where it had gone, but on 2 October news arrived that Nelson had located the fleet at anchor in Aboukir Bay and had destroyed it. But Napoleon's troops were now in Cairo and about to march northward. By December, Napoleon had subjugated most of Egypt and was marching into Palestine and heading towards Acre.

Now Grenville was more convinced that Smith should be sent on a diplomatic mission to Constantinople to deal with intelligence gathering and communication problems. His task was to strengthen Turkish opposition to Napoleon and to assist them in destroying the French army. He was appointed commander of HMS *Tigre* and told he could choose his crew. John Wright was selected, along with four of the French royalist friends who had helped Smith escape from Paris, Colonel Phélippeaux, François de Tromelin, Le Grand de Palluau, and Antoine Viscovitch, all of whom had taken commissions in the Turkish army.

On 21 October 1798, Smith also received his orders from the

Admiralty, which were to place himself under the command of the Earl of St Vincent in the Mediterranean.

As soon as this news reached Smith, he set sail from Alexandria in HMS *Tigre*, arriving at the walled city of Acre on 15 March 1799. Acre was of strategic importance to both Smith and Napoleon. Smith was fully aware that should Acre fall, then Napoleon would have a clear route to Constantinople. Seeing that the city would not be able to survive a French onslaught for long, Smith began to put it into a state of defence.

Napoleon's troops reached Acre a day after Smith. On 26 March, the French batteries opened fire, but their repeated assaults were driven back. Napoleon was far too impatient a man to endure a long siege, but Acre had to be captured. He was able to obtain reinforcements and expected Acre to fall either on 4 May or 5 May. Napoleon was skilled in warfare, but in Smith he had met his match.

By 7 May, the French siege guns had been sighted and another attack had been ordered following a two-day bombardment. Then, on the fifty-first day of the siege, the Turkish troops arrived by sea from Rhodes. Aware that ammunition and reinforcements were on their way, Napoleon ordered a very brutal attack that evening. Smith wrote to Napoleon about his "desire to avoid further bloodshed", saying that Acre had become stronger each day rather than having been weakened by two months under siege. Napoleon did not give up. Two more assaults followed, but the city walls were not breached. After discussions with Napoleon's generals, it was felt that the cost had been too expensive. Nor was it feasible to march northward and leave Acre uncaptured at their rear. Retreat was the only option, but a decision was taken for the remaining ammunition to be fired into Acre so that at least a claim could be made that the city had been destroyed if not captured.

Sir Sidney Smith at the Siege of Acre

On 20 May 1799, Smith watched from HMS *Tigre* as the French struck camp and prepared for their long march south. The following day, Smith, too, left, sailing for Jaffa aboard his ship. Napoleon's verdict on Smith was "That man made me miss my glory." Napoleon made his way back to Cairo with his demoralised army, depositing the sick and wounded at various French camps along the way, so that he could stage a triumphant entry into Cairo on 10 June. Smith tried to negotiate the surrender and repatriation of the remaining French forces under General Kléber. He signed the Convention of el-Arish, but because Nelson's view was that the French forces in Egypt should be annihilated, the British decided to send an army under Sir Ralph Abercromby to land at Aboukir Bay. This was the same man whom Richard had met and advised in November 1799 during the Anglo-Russian invasion of Holland.

Smith in the *Tigre* had sailed to Rhodes to advise a Turkish army which was gathering to assist the British in the reconquest of Egypt. The invasion, which took place on 8 March 1801, was successful, and the French were defeated, although there were heavy losses on both sides. At the Battle of Alexandria, Abercromby was wounded, later to die on 28 March. The Turks, though, had ignored Smith's advice about where to land and, after a successful beginning, suffered heavy losses.

On his return to England in 1801, Smith received some honours and a £1,000 pension for his services at Acre, but Nelson's victory at the Battle of Copenhagen put Smith's achievements into the shade, despite Nelson's being ostracised by high society for his affair with Emma Hamilton.

On 27 March 1802, France and Britain signed the Peace of Amiens, which temporarily ended the hostilities between them. Napoleon granted an amnesty to certain royalist émigrés, and some of them had returned to France. Several of them would be well known to Richard: Colonel Bromley, who had reverted to Tromelin; Captain Boisgirard; and Le Grand de Palluau.

Charles de Frotté did not return because his half-brother, General Louis de Frotté, a royalist commander in Normandy, had been shot on Napoleon's orders. John Wright had dared to return, despite being advised not to. He was captured and ended up back in the Temple, where more royalists were being imprisoned and tortured to ascertain the whereabouts of other leaders. Wright too was subjected to interrogation and ill-treatment and after eighteen months of capture it was announced that he had committed suicide in his cell. In Britain this was hotly disputed, and it was felt that he had almost certainly been murdered.

However, the continuing threat of invasion by Napoleon's Grande Armée led to the end of the treaty when, on 18 May 1803, Britain, now under Henry Addington as prime minister, decided to declare war on France.

Smith took command of the *Antelope* and kept watch in the North Sea as the French invasion forces moved south to concentrate between Ostend and Boulogne. His orders were to patrol and blockade. In 1804, he made some attacks on small craft. But his years of service in the Mediterranean had taken their toll. His health had begun to suffer so much that he asked for a transfer.

He now began to take an interest in new and innovative methods of warfare. He designed and built landing craft, making it easier for troops to be put ashore at low tide. On 15 October 1805, he attended Robert Fulton's latest trials at Walmer Castle in Kent, involving two of his mines which had been attached to a moored ship which had then been blown in two. Smith was impressed, but Lord St Vincent and Lord Keith were dismissive. Smith was, however, given permission to use Fulton's weapons in any future operations. He had made plans to attack Boulogne and Cadiz, but then news arrived that on 21 October the French and Spanish fleets had had been destroyed by Nelson off the coast of Trafalgar.

In November 1805, Smith was promoted to rear admiral. He sailed to the Mediterranean to join Nelson's successor, Lord Collingwood. He was given the task of helping King Ferdinand of the Two Sicilies retrieve the Kingdom of Naples from Napoleon's brother Joseph. In this, Smith was successful. On 4 July 1806, his troops defeated the much larger French army at the Battle of Maida.

Next Smith was sent to Constantinople in February 1807 to join an expedition led by Admiral Sir John Duckworth intended to prevent the French from forming an alliance with the Turks, under which they would be given free passage to Egypt. Duckworth kept Smith in a subordinate role, and the mission was a disaster with the British fleet being subjected to a Turkish onslaught as it retreated through the Dardanelles. Back in London, though, a positive spin was put on it.

On 27 October 1807, Napoleon signed a treaty with Spain to divide Portugal between them. In November, Smith was sent to Lisbon with secret orders. He had either to persuade Portugal to reverse their policy or to destroy their fleet and blockade Lisbon harbour. As the French army was approaching fast, Smith decided to escort the Portuguese fleet to Rio de Janeiro, which at the time was a Portuguese colony. Here he was involved in planning an attack on the Spanish colonies in South America, but he was recalled to Britain before any of his plans could come to fruition.

On 31 July 1810, Smith was promoted to vice admiral, and in October 1810 he married Caroline Rumbold, a widow, whose father, Sir George, had been involved with Smith in espionage work.

On 18 July 1812, Smith sailed again to the Mediterranean, tasked with maintaining a blockade on the port of Toulon. This was tedious work, with the French showing no signs of venturing out to fight. By now

Napoleon had begun the disastrous invasion of Russia. He would lose most of his Grande Armée in the winter retreat from Moscow. The French were beginning to crumble. In the Peninsula War, Napoleon's armies had been defeated by Wellington, who had crossed the Pyrenees into France in October 1813. That same month, Napoleon had been defeated at Leipzig by the Austrians, Russians, Prussians, and Swedish.

At the end of March 1814, the Allies entered Paris and the Napoleonic system collapsed, with Napoleon abdicating unconditionally on 11 April, to be exiled to Elba, off the Italian coast, on 4 May.

Smith returned to England on 1 July and involved himself in the antislavery cause, even attending the Congress of Vienna, which began in September 1814 and ran until June 1815. He campaigned for funds as well as military action to bring an end to slave-taking.

On 26 February 1815, Napoleon escaped from Elba and landed in France. On 20 March, he entered Paris and managed to raise an army of one hundred and twenty thousand men. King Louis XVIII fled. Knowing that the British, Austrians, Prussians, and Russians were preparing to wage war against him, Napoleon embarked upon his hundred-day campaign and marched his troops into Belgium. On Sunday, 18 June, he was beaten at Waterloo by an army of British, Belgian, Dutch, and German forces under the command of the Duke of Wellington and Field Marshal Blücher. Smith was on his way back from the Congress, and while travelling through Belgium just as the battle had finished, he managed to meet the Duke of Wellington and gave him his help in arranging for the surrender of the garrisons at Amiens and Arras. For his efforts, the Duke of Wellington awarded him a British knighthood—the insignia of the knight commander of the Order of the Bath.

Possibly like Richard, Smith had been enjoying a lavish lifestyle and living beyond his means. Aware of the British law's harshness towards debtors and of the possibility that he could well end up in prison, he decided to live abroad, setting up a home with his family in Paris. Whenever he spotted a suitable vacancy, he would apply to the Admiralty for an active role at sea. But he was never employed again. He probably took some pleasure, though, in hearing of the death of Napoleon from stomach cancer on the island of St Helena on 5 May 1821.

Smith enjoyed the social life in Paris and was renowned for his generosity and charity. His life was shattered with the death of his wife, Caroline, on 16 May 1826. As a widower, during his sixties and seventies he cut an increasingly eccentric but lovable character around Paris. He died of a stroke on 26 May 1840. He is buried with his wife in Pére Lachaise Cemetery.

There is no evidence that Smith ever again encountered Richard Cadman Etches.

CHAPTER 7

FINAL YEARS AND SUMMING UP

Richard's participation in the campaign to create a blockade in Boulogne harbour may well have been his final professional engagement as perhaps, at the age of fifty-one, his usefulness as a government agent may well have come to an end. This was certainly the opinion of the reviewer in the *Gentleman's Magazine*, which I referred to in the Introduction:

> Mr. Etches appears to have been honoured with the confidence of the government to a high degree, during the time when his utility was felt; but in common with many other political characters, he may have been forgotten when his services were less needed.

There is no doubt that his abortive plans caused some upset and embarrassment to people high up in the political, military, and naval world. He may never have worked for the government again.

From this point, around 1803 or 1804, his life seems to have taken a downward turn. Although during this period he was still resident at 19 Bryanston Street, Portman Square, London, he may have had difficulty maintaining the sort of lifestyle that he had been accustomed to.

The continuing war against France, which had begun in 1793 and lasted until Napoleon's defeat in 1815, had caused the British people great suffering from the heavy taxation and national debt that their government had imposed upon them. Initially, in 1793, the government had funded its own war effort and had even gone as far as to give contributions to other nations to encourage them to maintain their fight against the French.

But as the war continued and their funds dwindled, the government began to raise money by imposing the so-called "assessed taxes" on many luxury goods such as houses, carriages, servants, horses, and gold and silver plate. In time, the number of taxable items grew so large that it was said of the government, "Wherever you see an object, tax it!"

Added to this were two major turning points: in 1797, the Bank Restriction Act led the Bank of England to suspend its requirement to convert banknotes into gold to ease panic following fears of a French invasion, and in 1799, the prime minister, William Pitt, introduced income tax. How Richard was directly affected is not known, but records show that he had accumulated several debts which had caused him to be incarcerated in gaol. The discharge books for the King's Bench and Fleet Prison show that he repaid debts on 26 May 1803, 22 May 1805, and 7 October 1806. In February 1805, he was sued by one of his former partners, Daniel Beale. Had the Nootka Sound venture ended in financial disaster for him?

The Fleet Prison, which had been built as long ago as 1197, was situated just off the Farringdon road, just outside the city walls, and was the first building in London to be specifically designed as a gaol. It is arguably the best known of London's debtor prisons. During its lifetime, its buildings were destroyed three times: firstly, during the Peasants' Revolt in 1381, then in the Great Fire of London in 1666, and finally in the Gordon Riots of 1780.

The prison housed about three hundred debtors and their families. It was a prison for those convicted under the Star Chamber or Court of Chancery, and like other prisons in London, it was a profit-making enterprise with harsh punishments being meted out to those inmates who could not pay their dues. Fees were levied for turning keys, for putting on irons, and fees taking them off again. Even visitors paid fees. The Fleet Prison's fees were the highest in the whole of England. Provided they paid the keeper for his loss of earnings, it was perfectly acceptable for inmates to take lodgings nearby rather than stay in the prison.

Until several acts were passed in the 1860s, it was common for individuals to be jailed for debt or bankruptcy in debtors' prisons. Those who faced insolvency often found themselves in prison indefinitely. They had to pay their debts to be released, and since they also had to pay for their keep and could pay for extra freedoms, such as living in the "Rules"—areas just outside the prison walls—their stays could be lengthy unless they had family to pay the debts.

Prisoners who had a trade might continue to work and earn while being held at the Fleet, but most were reduced to begging. To pay for their keep, it was not unusual for inmates to beg from their cell windows or from the "grille" facing the street on the Farringdon side of the prison.

Racquet Yard at Fleet Prison

On 27 February 1729, the recently formed Gaols Committee visited the prison and were appalled at the conditions the prisoners were living in and the ill treatment they received. Among them, the committee members found Sir William Rich, a baronet, held in irons. Unable to pay a prison fee, he had been burned with a red-hot poker and kept in a dungeon for ten days for having wounded the warden with a shoemaker's knife. Further investigations led to the keeper, Thomas Bambridge, and his predecessor, John Huggins, being accused of extortion and murder. Although both were eventually acquitted, a special Act of Parliament was passed to dismiss Bambridge from his post.

By now attitudes towards debtors had begun to change. Debtors were freed when the plaintiff's opportunity to render a case against the defendant had expired, when the debt was paid off (usually through charitable means), or if the prisoner was freed in accordance with one of the frequent Insolvent Debtors' Acts. Other prisons were created, and conditions at the Fleet gradually deteriorated. It was closed in 1842 and sold to the Corporation of the City of London in 1844, who demolished it in 1846.

Although the foregoing events happened many years before Richard's incarceration, there is no reason to believe that the conditions he endured had improved in the interim. While it is true that by the end of the eighteenth century attitudes towards debtors had begun to change, conditions at the Fleet had deteriorated further. The final years of Richard's life must have been spent in wretched misery.

Richard died in the prison on Friday, 30 May 1817. A coroner's inquest was held there on the following Monday, 2 June, at which Richard's sister Sally, of Aldersgate Street, made a sworn statement in which she said that he had been a prisoner for debt and had been held for "about two months or more before his death". She added that Richard had been "in a declining state of heath for a considerable length of time". People attended him at prison for a month before his death, and he had "medical of every proper assistance but he died last Friday a natural death by a visit of God".

The verdict of the coroner, Thomas Shelton, was:

> Richard Cadman Etches being a prisoner in the said prison of the Fleet on the 30th day of May in the year aforesaid and long before that day to-wit for the space of two months and more was and had been sick and diseased on his body and of such sickness and disease at the parish and ward aforesaid did languish and languishing did live and that Richard Cadman Etches on the said thirtieth day of May that year aforesaid did at the parish and ward aforesaid of the said sickness and disease did die a natural death by the visitation of God.

George Weatherfield No. 523.	Lambeth	May 25	59	M West
Louisa Catharine Myear No. 524.	Shoe Lane	May 25	24	M West
Ann Jackson No. 525.	WorkHouse	May 26	30	M West
Richard Cadman Etches No. 526.	Fleet Prison	June 2	52	M West
Mary Tagg No. 527.	St Dunstans West	June 7	61	M West
Mary Barden No. 528.	Salisbury Square	June 10	39	M Binder

The Record of Richard's Burial

Richard was buried at the nearby St Bride's Church on 2 June 1817. The burial note gives his abode as Fleet Prison. His age is shown as fifty-two, but I believe this is an error. He would have been sixty-three. Unfortunately, the church was hit by a German bomb in World War II and the graves were destroyed.

William Etches, Richard's older brother, who had earlier been in partnership with him as a wine merchant, had by 1784 moved to Sheep Street, Northampton, where he carried on the same trade. On 24 October 1785, he married Mary Clifford. They had three sons, John, George, and William. Mary died in 1788, probably after the birth of her third son. In 1789 William married again, to Ellen Litton.

In 1793 William was declared bankrupt, and on 7 November at the Peacock Inn, Northampton, an auction of his property took place. But two years later, in February 1795, he announced that he was to open a warehouse at Holborn Hill, London, from which he intended to supply the "Nobility, Shopkeepers and the Public in general" with "tea, grocery and compounds". It seems that this venture was unsuccessful because, by the time of his father's death in 1795, he had moved back to Ashbourne, where he and Ellen had three more children. He died in 1839.

Richard's younger brother John, who had travelled to the Northwest

Coast with James Colnett, continued to live in London with his wife, Sarah, whom he had married at St Andrew's, Holborn, on 13 February 1774. Little is known of his subsequent life, but the couple possibly had three children, all daughters, of whom only one, Sarah, survived into adulthood. John died in 1818.

Summing Up

Richard lived from 1753 until 1817, dying at the age of sixty-three. He lived through a period which is arguably unsurpassed in history. During his lifetime, he witnessed the loss of the American colonies, the collapse of the Spanish Empire in America, the French Revolution, and Wellington's and Nelson's great victories over Napoleon.

Not only that, but he played a not insignificant part himself, much of it unnoticed. This is understandable as for much of his life he operated as a British agent, nearly always abroad and working under cover. He lived and worked in keeping with the code of the intelligence agents, which was "to work unobtrusively in the tradition of accomplishment and anonymity".

Before that he had carved out a successful career in the City of London and was extremely well connected as can be seen from his correspondence and from those who came into his life. He was fortunate enough to live in exciting but sometimes exceedingly dangerous times. While life in London for the successful and well connected in the late eighteenth century was beneficial, it was also a frightening period because of the constant threat of invasion by the French from 1793 to 1815. Europe was at war during this whole period with just one year of peace, after the Treaty of Amiens was signed in 1802.

But they were great days, stirring days, and Richard had his full share in those events. He took great risks in sending ships to the Northwest Coast to trade. How must he have felt when the capture of one his ships almost caused Britain to go to war with Spain? He risked his life as a British agent operating in Europe in dangerous times. His role in the escape of Sir Sidney Smith was no doubt the highlight of his career in espionage, but there were other great triumphs too, and not only in espionage.

He was a friend of Sir Joseph Banks, and he was associated with many influential people in the British government, the army, and the navy, as well as in the City of London.

He lived in the Age of Enlightenment, an age of new thought and of commerce and exploration, and he played a full part. The foregoing chapters make it clear that no inconsiderable share in the defence of his country and its victories over its enemies, which came to the British in those unsettled days, can be attributed to the ability, zeal, and courage of this remarkable man.

I hope that this book will in some way do justice to his memory.

CHRONOLOGY OF PRINCIPAL EVENTS

Chronology of Principal Events

Year	Richard Cadman Etches (RCE) and Domestic Events	(RCE) and Historical Events in the Rest of the World
1743	24 February—Birth of Joseph Banks in Soho, London	
1744	Birth year of RCE according to Robert Galois, editor of James Colnett's journals	
1745	The Jacobite rebellion led by the "Young Pretender", Charles Edward Stuart, takes place 21 September—The Jacobites defeat a government army at Prestonpans 3 December—The "Young Pretender" and his Jacobite army arrive in Ashbourne	
1746	16 April—The Jacobites are defeated at the Battle of Culloden Moor	
1747		
1748	Births of Nathaniel Portlock and George Dixon	
1749		
1750		
1751		
1752	1 September—Marriage of RCE's parents, William Etches and Elizabeth Cadman, at Tutbury, Staffordshire	

1753	2 November—RCE baptised at Shipston-on-Stour, Warwickshire Birth of James Colnett in Devonport, Devon	
1754		
1755	17 June—James Cook joins the Royal Navy 8 September—William Etches (RCE's brother) baptised at Shipston-on-Stour, Warwickshire	
1756	Possible year of John Meares's birth in Dublin, Ireland	Start of Seven Years War (1756-1763) involving Great Britain, Prussia, France, Austria, and Russia
1757	22 June—Birth of George Vancouver in King's Lynn, Norfolk 20 July—John Etches (RCE's brother) baptised at Shipston-on-Stour, Warwickshire	
1758	29 September—Birth of Horatio Nelson in Burnham Thorpe, Norfolk	
1759	28 May—Birth of William Pitt the Younger at Hayes, Kent	
1760	October—George III ascends to the throne	
1761	Birth and death of Jane Etches (RCE's sister) in Ashbourne, Derbyshire 22 September—George III is crowned king	

1762	13 March—Birth of Elizabeth Etches (RCE's sister) in Ashbourne, Derbyshire 21 December—James Cook marries Elizabeth Batts at Barking, Essex
1763	16 April—George Grenville becomes prime minister
1764	Invention of the spinning jenny by James Hargreaves, Lancashire which increased production of cotton 21 June—Birth of William Sidney Smith in Westminster, London Prime minister George Grenville introduces Stamp Act as means of raising revenue in American colonies
1765	22 March—Stamp Act passed Birth year of RCE if he died at age fifty-two
1766	30 July—William Pitt the Elder becomes prime minister
1767	
1768	Birth of Lydia Etches (RCE's sister) in Ashbourne, Derbyshire 1 August—Start of James Cook's first voyage aboard HMS *Endeavour*. Joseph Banks is part of expedition
1769	1 May—Birth of Arthur Wellesley (later Duke of Wellington) in Dublin, Ireland 15 August—Birth of Napoleon Bonaparte in Ajaccio, Corsica
1770	28 January—Lord North becomes prime minister Death of Lydia Etches in Ashbourne, Derbyshire. Buried 9 December 28 April—James Cook and HMS *Endeavour* arrive in Botany Bay, Australia

1771	12 July—James Cook returns to England from his first voyage	
	August—James Cook promoted to commander	
1772	13 July—Start of James Cook's second voyage aboard HMS *Resolution*	
1773		17 January—Cook crosses the Antarctic circle for the first time in history and explores the region
1774		Cook returns to New Zealand before making his journey home to England
		Louis XV dies. His grandson succeeds him as King Louis XVI
1775	29 May—Birth of Sarah Etches (RCE's sister) in Ashbourne, Derbyshire	19 April/June—American Revolutionary War begins
	30 July—Cook returns to England in HMS *Resolution*	
	November—RCE and his brother William trading as wine and spirit merchants in London and Ashbourne	
1776	12 July—James Cook sails from Plymouth on his third and final voyage	
1777		
1778	30 November—Joseph Banks elected president of the Royal Society	18 January—Cook discovers the Sandwich Islands, now known as the Hawaiian Islands
		29 March—James Cook in HMS *Resolution* arrives at Nootka Sound
		26 April—James Cook leaves Nootka Sound

1779	March—Joseph Banks marries Dorothea Hugessen RCE enters partnership with Robert Hanning Brooks to trade as tea and wine merchants	14 February—Death of James Cook at Kealakekua Bay, Hawaii
1780	11 January—The *London Gazette* announces Cook's death June—The Anti-Catholic Gordon Riots take place in London 4 October—James Cook's vessels *Resolution* and *Discovery* return to London	April—Captain Jonathan Haraden captures the *Golden Eagle* in the Bay of Biscay
1781	4 September—RCE made free by redemption from Carpenter's Company	October—Great Britain surrenders to the Americans at Battle of Yorktown
1782	Evan Nepean sets up system of spy surveillance	
1783	RCE joins the Carpenter's Company as liveryman RCE recruited by Catherine of Russia James Matra proposes the establishment of a penal colony in New South Wales and the development of trade in the Pacific 19 December—William Pitt the Younger becomes prime minister	3 September—Treaty of Paris signed, bringing an end to the American Revolutionary War. It recognised the United States and ceded Florida to Spain
1784	Publication of James Cook's journals	

1785	13 March—RCE meets Joseph Banks March—RCE draws up plans for sea otter trade on the North Pacific coast RCE fits out *King George* and *Queen Charlotte* King George's Sound Company founded by RCE August/ September—East India Company and South Sea Company agree to grant licences for RCE to trade 29 August—*King George* and *Queen Charlotte* sail from Deptford dock 3 September—RCE's letter sets out instructions for Nathaniel Portlock and George Dixon as they journey to the Northwest Coast	
1786	1 September—RCE's South Sea Company licence issued for a period of five years 23 September—*Prince of Wales* and *Princess Royal* sail from Deptford dock	20 January—John Meares purchases *Nooka* and *Sea Otter* 24 May—*King George* and *Queen Charlotte* arrive in Kealakekua Bay, Hawaii 29 May—John Meares sails from Malacca to Macao 1 August—John Meares sights the Aleutian Islands

1787	21 April—*Duke of York* sails from London	May—John Meares and his crew are rescued by George Dixon 22 June—John Meares departs for Macao 4 July—*Prince of Wales* and *Princess Royal* arrive in Nootka Sound 11 September—*Duke of York* lost at sea, off Tierra del Fuego 1 October—*Columbia Rediviva* and *Lady Washington* sail from Boston to the Northwest Coast 20 October—John Meares arrives at Macao December—Portlock and Dixon arrive at Canton
1788	August/ September—Portlock and Dixon arrive back in England from RCE's first voyage Summer—George III shows signs of mental illness	January—John Meares forms Merchant Proprietors Company 22 January—*Felice Adventurer* and *Iphigenia Nubiana* are fitted out and depart from Macao to Nootka Sound 13 May – Meares and *Felice Adventurer* arrive at Nootka Sound 31 January—Death of Charles Edward Stuart in Rome 16 September—*Lady Washington* under Robert Gray arrives at Nootka Sound 19 September—*North West America* launched 22 September—*Columbia Rediviva* under John Kendrick arrives at Nootka Sound 24 September—John Meares sails for Canton in *Felice Adventurer* 5 December—John Meares arrives in Macao

1789	23 January—RCE merges with John Meares and Associated Merchants is formed
	24 April—*Iphigenia Nubiana* returns to Nootka Sound
	26 April—James Colnett sails in the *Argonaut* from Macao to Nootka Sound
	5 May—Martínez arrives at Nootka Sound in *Princesa*
	12 May—de Haro arrives at Nootka Sound in *San Carlos*
	15 June—Thomas Hudson arrives at Nootka Sound in *Princess Royal*
	2 July—James Colnett and *Argonaut* arrive at Nootka Sound as Hudson departs
	4 July—James Colnett arrested and sent to San Blas
	14 July—Paris mob storms the Bastille. The French Revolution begins
	September—RCE orders boarding of *Isabella*
	14 September—*Isabella* boarded and sailed into Ostend
	5 October—William Douglas and *Iphigenia* arrive at Macao
	17 November—Robert Gray arrives in *Columbia Rediviva*
	5 December—John Meares leaves Macao for London
	December—RCE employed as a British secret service agent and residing in Calais, France
	While in Copenhagen RCE achieves Danish nationality

1790	4 January—British government learns about James Colnett's arrest and seizure of his vessel. The Nootka Sound crisis begins April—John Meares returns to England with his Memorial 13 May—Meares's Memorial presented to Parliament 27 May—John Meares addresses the Privy Committee for Trade July—William Pitt sends fresh threat to Spain 14 October—William Pitt sends Spain an ultimatum 26 November—Announcement of peace with Spain made in Parliament RCE issues a petition to be pardoned against a charge of piracy	25 January—Spain issues protest to British government May—James Colnett released by the Spaniards 9 July—James Colnett is permitted to sail 24 July—Spain accepts British demands over Nootka 28 October—First Nootka Sound Convention established in Madrid Russia and Austria declare war on the Ottoman Empire
1791	22 March—RCE signs affidavit before John Boydell, Mayor of London, regarding a charge of piracy 1 April—George Vancouver sails from Falmouth in HMS *Discovery* 1 April—The Butterworth Squadron prepares to sail from London to the Northwest Coast 11 July—William Etches writes to Evan Nepean regarding progress on RCE's piracy petition	20–21 June—Louis XVI and Marie Antoinette flee Paris but are arrested at Varennes. Louis accepts the new constitution

| 1792 | 19 May—RCE complains to Joseph Banks about Dixon and Portlock

30 July—Sir Ralph Woodford forwards RCE and John Meares's letter to Henry Dundas re: furs aboard *Hindostan*

25 August—Letter from RCE and John Meares about East India Company's procrastination

11 September—RCE receives letter from Sir Ralph Woodford about sea otter furs and reluctantly accepts East India Company's offer

21 November—Aliens Bill introduced by British government

Spy surveillance system being run by William Clarke and twelve assistants. | 29 March—King Gustav of Sweden is assassinated while at the Royal Opera House, Stockholm

April—France is declared a republic

20 April—France declares war on Austria, Prussia, and Piedmont

10 August—March on the Tuileries; Louis XVI deposed and taken prisoner

31 August—Massacres begin in Paris

21 September—Establishment of French First Republic and National Convention |

1793	7 January—Aliens Act becomes law in reaction to anxiety over large number of refugees entering Britain towards the end of 1792, mainly from France 1 February—Nelson put in command of HMS *Agamemnon* April—Nelson sails to the Mediterranean to join Lord Hood's fleet in blocking French fleet in Toulon 7 November—William Erches declared bankrupt	21 January—Louis XVI guillotined at the Place de la Concorde, Paris. Exiled French royalists declare Louis XVII king 1 February—France declares war on Britain 7 February—France declares war on Spain 12 February—Second Nootka Convention signed 13 February—First Coalition formed—Britain, Austria, Prussia, Netherlands, Sardinia-Piedmont, Spain 27 August—Lord Hood occupies Toulon 5 September—The Reign of Terror begins in France 16 October—Marie Antoinette guillotined at the Place de la Concorde, Paris 19 December—Napoleon captures Toulon. Smith sets fire to the French fleet. Hood sails to Corsica
1794	15 January—Sidney Smith given command of HMS *Diamond*	11 January—Third Nootka Convention signed in Madrid. Known as the "Convention for the Mutual Abandonment of Nootka" June/July—Height of The Reign of Terror in Paris 28 July—Robespierre guillotined at the Place de la Concorde, Paris. The Reign of Terror draws to a close August–November—French advance in Netherlands; French occupation of Amsterdam 2 December—George Vancouver begins homeward journey from the North Pacific

1795	26 February—John Meares promoted to commander in the Royal Navy and made a baronet	January—French troops conquer the Netherlands
	28 March—Spain's banner at Nootka Sound taken down	28 March—Spain's banner at Nootka Sound taken down
	9 June—Death of William Etches (RCE's father) in Ashbourne, Derbyshire	May—Sir William Eden arrives in Dieppe to negotiate prisoner exchange on behalf of British government
	20 October—George Vancouver arrives back in England	June—RCE arrives in Paris for discussions about prisoner exchange and secures release of 12,000 men
	November—Riots take place in Britain over high price of bread and wheat	8 June—Louis XVII dies uncrowned in the Temple prison, Paris
	December—Treasonable Practices and Seditious Meetings Acts approved following stoning of George III on his way to open Parliament	13 June—Napoleon is promoted to General of the Army of the West
		22 August—The Directory replaces the Jacobin regime in Paris
		5 October—13 Vendémiare. Napoleon orders cannonade on royalist army in Paris. RCE sustains an injury
		October—Rebellion in the Vendée crushed, ending hopes of early restoration of the Bourbon monarchy. Napoleon tasked with suppressing civil strife and rebellion against the Republic
		2 November—The Directory comes to power following the end of the Reign of Terror
		December—RCE returns to Paris

1796	March—Insurrection Act. Provides authority to stamp out agitation caused by United Irishmen	23 February—Napoleon is given command of the French Army of Italy
	7 May—RCE writes to Lord Spencer with a plan for communicating military intelligence	11 March—The Italian campaign against Austria begins
	RCE returns from Holland with information for Evan Nepean	10 May—Napoleon defeats Austrian forces at the Battle of Lodi
		17 April—Smith captured and imprisoned by the French
		3 July—Smith, Wright and Bromley transferred to the Temple prison, Paris
		19 August—Treaty signed between France and Spain uniting them against Britain
		8 October—Spain declares war on Britain
		22 October—Earl of Malmesbury arrives in France to negotiate Sidney Smith's release
		17 November—Napoleon defeats Austrian forces at the Battle of Arcole
		17 November—Death of Catherine the Great of Russia in Saint Petersburg. Her son, Paul, becomes emperor

1797	22 February—Bank Restriction Act: Bank of England suspends requirement to convert banknotes into gold to ease panic following rumours of a French invasion 16 April—Spithead mutiny begins mainly concerning grievances over Royal Navy pay RCE goes to Holland to spy on navy/military and submits plan to British government upon his return 24 November—William Pitt's finance bill proposes income tax and other indirect taxes	14 January—Napoleon defeats large Austrian army at the Battle of Rivoli 14 February—Battle of St Vincent: Admiral Jervis defeats Spanish off Cape St Vincent. Nelson distinguishes himself and becomes a national hero 12 May—Napoleon brings the Republic of Venice to an end 22–23 July—Nelson unsuccessfully attacks a Spanish treasure ship at Santa Cruz de Tenerife. He loses an arm. 4 September—Coup d'état of 18 Fructidor 11 October—Admiral Duncan defeats Dutch fleet at Battle of Camperdown 17 October—Napoleon signs the Treaty of Campo Formio with Austria 5 December—Napoleon returns to Paris as a hero
1798	7 May—Sidney Smith returns to England 10 May—George Vancouver dies in obscurity in Petersham 23 May—Irish Rebellion begins 21 October—Sidney Smith sails to the Mediterranean aboard HMS *Tigre* 3 December—William Pitt introduces income tax at 10%, exempting incomes below £60	24 April—Sidney Smith escapes from the Temple prison 19 May—Napoleon leaves Toulon with an army of 38,000 to begin his Egyptian campaign June—Napoleon occupies Malta 3 July—Napoleon lands in Alexandria 21 July—Napoleon wins a decisive victory against the Mamelukes at the Battle of the Pyramids 24 July—The fall of Cairo 1 August—the British fleet under Nelson's command defeats the French navy at the Battle of the Nile 24 December—Anglo-Russian Treaty signed

1799	February—Napoleon leaves Cairo for Syria 7 March—French troops occupy Jaffa 12 March—France declares war on Austria 15 March—Sidney Smith arrives at Acre 26 March—Napoleon begins Siege of Acre 20 May—Sidney Smith relieves Acre 1 June—Second Coalition formed: Britain, Russia, Austria, Portugal, Turkey, and the Two Sicilies against France 16 June—Spain declares war on Britain 23 August—Napoleon leaves Alexandria for France 27 August/19 November—RCE commands a flotilla of small boats off Texel 2 October – Battle of Alkmaar 12 December—Napoleon is elected First Consul of the Consulate
1800	January—Britain suffers from food shortages. Soup kitchens are set up in London and provincial towns March—Act of Union with Ireland passed in Dublin and Westminster 6 May—French army marches to Italy; Napoleon crosses Alps 14 June—Napoleon defeats Austrian forces at the Battle of Marengo 23 August—Napoleon leaves Alexandria to return to France 29 August—British fleet arrives off Copenhagen 16 December—Sweden, Denmark, and Russia form League of Armed Neutrality, hostile to Britain 24 December—Royalist rebels attempt to assassinate Napoleon with a bomb on his way to the opera

174

1801	1 January—Act of Union between Britain and Ireland comes into force 5 February—George III accepts Pitt's resignation 8 March—Sidney Smith returns to England 16 February—William Pitt resigns 17 March—Henry Addington succeeds him as prime minister 19 March—Henry Addington's government sues for peace 1 October – Peace preliminaries signed in London	21 March—British army under Sir Ralph Abercromby win decisive victory against the French at the Battle of Alexandria. Abercromby is mortally wounded and dies on 28 March 24 March—Assassination of Tsar Paul. Treaty of Armed Neutrality is shattered 2 April—The British fleet under Nelson defeat Danish forces at the Battle of Copenhagen. The Danish navy is destroyed 3, 4 and 15 August—Nelson unsuccessfully attacks Boulogne 2 September—French surrender in Egypt
1802	Etches v. Beale court case is heard at Leicester assizes July/August—General election is held in Britain	27 March—Peace of Amiens signed bringing peace in Europe for 14 months during the Napoleonic Wars 2 August—Napoleon is made First Consul for life
1803	18 May—Britain declares war on France	
1804	15 February—RCE is involved in building "stone ships" with which to prevent the French fleet from leaving Boulogne harbour 10 May—Henry Addington's government resigns 10 May—William Pitt returns to office 20 July—William Pitt meets with Robert Fulton to discuss unconventional weaponry 11 August—RCE discloses Napoleon's invasion plans to British government George III suffers a second major bout of insanity	12 April—The "stone ships" arrive at the mouth of Boulogne harbour 21 March—The Napoleonic Code is introduced July—Napoleon sites himself at Boulogne and plans to attack England 2 December—Napoleon crowns himself emperor. His civil code is adopted 12 December—Spain joins France and declares war on Britain, raising the threat of a combined invasion

1805	11 January—Britain declares war on Spain 15 October—Sidney Smith attends Robert Fulton's weapon trials at Walmer Castle November—Sidney Smith promoted to rear admiral	17 March—Napoleon becomes king of the newly formed Italian Republic 29 March—French fleet under Admiral Villeneuve breaks out of Toulon 22 July—Battle of Cape Finisterre. Villeneuve retreats to Cadiz 21 October—Britain fights combined French and Spanish fleets at the Battle of Trafalgar. Nelson is killed 2 December—Napoleon defeats Austria and Russia at the Battle of Austerlitz—his greatest victory
1806	9 January—Nelson's funeral. He is laid to rest in St Paul's Cathedral 23 January—Death of William Pitt at Putney Heath, London 11 February—William Grenville becomes prime minister and forms Whig "Ministry of All the Talents" 1 September—Death of James Colnett at Great Ormond St., London 13 September—Charles Fox dies and is succeeded by Charles, 2nd Earl Grey, as leader of the Foxite Whigs	5 July—Napoleon is proclaimed king of Holland 27 October—Napoleon enters Berlin having defeated Prussia at the Battle of Jena 28 November—French army enters Warsaw

| 1807 | February—Sidney Smith sails to Constantinople to prevent a French alliance with Turkey

25 March—Lord Grenville's ministry resigns. Duke of Portland forms Tory government. Slave Trade Bill gains royal assent | 18 March—British forces under General Mackenzie-Fraser invade Egypt but are defeated at the Battle of Rosetta

14 June—Napoleon defeats a large Russian force at the Battle of Friedland

7 July—Tsar Alexander makes peace with Napoleon in the Treaty of Tilsit and forms an alliance with France

August–September—British attack on Copenhagen leads to surrender of Danish/Norwegian fleet

26 October—Russia declares war on Britain

27 October—Treaty of Fontainebleau signed by France and Spain to divide Portugal between them

19/30 November—Beginning of French occupation of Portugal

29 November—Sir Sidney Smith's squadron escorts Portuguese royal family and fleet to Brazil before French attack

22 December—Embargo Act passed by US Congress placing a trade embargo on all foreign nations |

1808	2 February—French occupy Rome 27 February—French troops invade Spain under General Junot May—Napoleon proclaims his brother, Joseph Bonaparte, king of Spain 21 August—Arthur Wellesley given command of British army in Portugal defeats Junot at the Battle of Vimeiro 30 August—Convention of Cintra. Controversial agreement allows French to evacuate Portugal without further conflict 4 December—Madrid surrenders to Napoleon	10 May—British troops under Sir John Moore sent to Sweden to assist King Gustavus IV, but following disagreements, they return on 15 July 12 July—Arthur Wellesley sails to Portugal with nine thousand troops
1809	1 January—Napoleon leaves Spain for Paris 5 January—Treaty of Dardenelles agreed, ending the Anglo-Turkish war 16–17 January—Battle of Corunna, Spain. French army, under Marshal Soult force British troops to withdraw. Sir John Moore is mortally wounded 22 April—Arthur Wellesley assumes command of British troops in Portugal 12 May—Arthur Wellesley defeats Marshall Soult at the Battle of Porto. The French army withdraws from Portugal 13 May—Napoleon enters Vienna 4 July—Arthur Wellesley enters Spain 27 July—Arthur Wellesley defeats French army at the Battle of Talavera, Spain 5–6 July—Napoleon defeats Austria at the Battle of Wagram 26 August—Arthur Wellesley is elevated to the peerage as Viscount Wellington	29 January—Death of John Meares in Bath, possibly aged fifty-three 21 September—Government ministers Canning and Castlereagh fight a duel on Putney Heath. Both survive but resign from the Cabinet 4 October—Spencer Perceval succeeds the Duke of Portland as prime minister 25 October—George III's Golden Jubilee is celebrated 30 October—Death of Duke of Portland. Spencer Perceval succeeds him as prime minister

1810	31 July—Sidney Smith promoted to vice admiral October—Sidney Smith marries Caroline Rumbold December—George III becomes dangerously ill	17 February—Napoleon annexes Rome to his French empire 1 April—Napoleon marries Archduchess Marie-Louise of Austria 9 July—The Netherlands is annexed to the French empire 17 November—Sweden declares war on Britain 13 December—French annexe north-west Germany (Hamburg, Bremen, Lubeck, and Hanover) to the French empire 31 December—Tsar Alexander 1 opens Russian ports to neutral vessels
1811	5 February—Regency Act. Prince of Wales becomes regent because of George III's illness	May—Wellington has further successes in Spain

179

1812	11 May—Prime minister Spencer Perceval is assassinated	January—French troops leave Spain in preparation for Russian campaign
	8 June—Lord Liverpool becomes prime minister	19 January—Wellington takes Ciudad Rodrigo
	18 July—Sidney Smith sails to the Mediterranean to maintain the Toulon blockade	16 March—Wellington besieges Badajoz
		7 April—Badajoz falls to Wellington
		22-23 July—Wellington wins decisive Battle of Salamanca and is created Earl of Wellington
		18 June—United States declares war on Britain
		24 June—Napoleon begins invasion of Russia
		12 August—Wellington enters Madrid
		16–17 August—Napoleon leads French victory over Russians at the Battle of Smolensk
		7 September—France and Russia fight the Battle of Borodino. Result is inconclusive as both sides sustain huge losses
		14 September—Napoleon's Grande Armée enters Moscow but finding the city abandoned retreats, suffering devastating losses
		19–22 September—Wellington besieges Burgos but is forced to retreat with two thousand casualties
		19 October—Napoleon begins retreat of Grande Armée from Moscow
		5 December—Napoleon leaves his retreating army and returns to Paris to raise forces

1813	July—Charter Act passed. East India Company's charter is renegotiated resulting in the loss of their commercial monopoly.	13 March—Russians enter Berlin 17 March—Prussia declares war on France May—French leave Madrid. Napoleon wins narrow victories in battles at Lutzen and Bautzen 21 June—Combined British, Spanish and Portuguese army under Wellington defeat French at Battle of Vittoria and drive French from northern Spain 26–27 August—Napoleon defeats Allies at Battle of Dresden 8 October—Wellington's army enters France 16–19 October—Napoleon defeated at "Battle of the Nations" at Leipzig and is compelled to return to France 10 November—Wellington wins the Battle of Nivelle. Napoleon enters France 24 December—Allies besiege Hamburg

1814	January—Allies invade France	June—Tsar Alexander; Frederick, King of Prussia; Prince Metternich; Field Marshall Blücher and other dignitaries visit England to celebrate peace and Napoleon's abdication
	25 March—Combined Allied armies march on Paris	July—Sidney Smith returns to England and becomes involved in the anti-slavery cause
	30–31 March—The Allies enter Paris. General Marmont surrenders to them	
	10 April—Wellington and Allies win Battle of Toulouse	
	11 April—Treaty of Fontainebleau signed, ending Napoleon's rule as emperor	
	11 April—Napoleon abdicates and is exiled to Elba. Louis XVIII becomes king	
	3 May—Louis XVIII restores the Bourbon monarchy	
	4 May—Napoleon arrives on Elba. His wife and son take refuge in Vienna	
	30 May—First Treaty of Paris signed, bringing an end to the war of the Sixth Coalition	
	September—Congress of Vienna opens to withdraw the map of Europe	
	24 December—Treaty of Ghent ends Anglo-American War of 1812	

1815	March—Passing of Corn Laws increasing the price of grain causes riots in London 6 April—American naval prisoners cause riots in Dartmoor Prison following delay in their release	8 January—British defeated at New Orleans before peace declaration is known 26 February—Napoleon escapes from Elba to land in France on 1 March 20 March—Napoleon reaches Paris. Start of the Hundred Days War 9 June—Treaty of Vienna signed, committing allied powers to fight until Napoleon is again defeated 15 June—Napoleon invades Belgium 18 June—Battle of Waterloo. French defeated by Blücher and Wellington 22 June—Napoleon abdicates 28 June—Restoration of Louis XVIII 15 July—Napoleon surrenders to British at the port of Rochefort 16 October—Napoleon exiled to the island of Saint Helena 20 November—Second Treaty of Paris ends the French War
1816		
1817	30 May—RCE dies of natural causes in Fleet Prison, aged sixty-three 2 June – RCE is buried at St. Bride's Church, London 12 September—Death of Nathaniel Portlock in Greenwich, London	
1818	Death of John Etches (RCE's brother)	
1819		
1820	29 January—George III dies at Windsor Castle	
1821		5 May—Napoleon dies on the island of St Helena

BIBLIOGRAPHY

Adkins, Roy and Lesley, *The War for all the Oceans* (Viking Penguin, 2007).

Bown, Stephen R., *Madness, Betrayal, and the Lash* (Douglas & McIntyre, 2008).

British Columbia Quarterly Review (April 1942).

Collingridge, Vanessa, *Captain Cook: Obsession and Betrayal in the New World* (Ebury Press, Random House, 2003).

Dawson and Hobson, *The History and Topography of Ashbourn* (1839).

Denton, V. L., *The Far West Coast* (J. M. Dent & Sons, 1924).

Dixon, George, *Remarks on the Voyages of John Meares* (Forgotten Books, 2012).

Durey, Michael, *The British Secret Service and the Escape of Sir Sidney Smith from Paris in 1798* (The Historical Association, 1999)

Earle, James, *Commodore Squib: The Life, Times and Secretive Wars of England's First Rocket Man, Sir William Congreve, 1772-1828* (Cambridge Scholars Publishing, 2010)

Etches, Charles W., *The Life and Adventures of Richard Cadman Etches of Ashbourne, Derbyshire Shipowner, and Fur Trader on the North West Coast of America (1785–1789), Navy Intelligence Agent on the Continent during the Napoleonic Wars* (Unpublished manuscript, New York, 1950).

Galois, Robert M., ed., *A Voyage to the North West Side of America: The Journals of James Colnett, 1786–89* (UBC Press, 2004).

Gough, Barry M., *Distant Dominion: Britain and the Northwest Coast of North America, 1579–1809* (University of British Columbia Press, 1980).

Haigh, William, *William Pitt the Younger* (Harper Press, 2005).

Holmes, Richard, *The Age of Wonder* (Harper Press, 2008).

Hough, Richard, *Captain James Cook* (Hodder and Stoughton, 1994).

Knight, Roger, *Britain against Napoleon: The Organization of Victory, 1783–1815* (Penguin, 2014).

Mackay, David, *In the wake of Cook- Exploration, Science, and Empire, 1780-1801* (Croom Helm Ltd., 1985)

McLynn, Frank, *Napoleon, A Biography* (Pimlico, 1998).

Moore, Peter, *Endeavour: The Ship that Changed the World* (Farrar, Strauss, and Giroux, 2019).

Nokes, J. Richard, *Almost a Hero: The Voyages of John Meares, R.N., to China, Hawaii, and the Northwest Coast* (Washington State University Press, 1998).

Pocock, Tom, *A Thirst for Glory: The Life of Admiral Sir Sidney Smith* (Pimlico, 1998).

Porter, Roy, *English Society in the 18th Century* (Pelican, 1982).

Ridley, Scott, *Morning of Fire* (William Morrow, 2010).

Rigby, Nigel, Pieter van der Merwe, and Glyn Williams, *Pioneers of the Pacific: Voyages of Exploration, 1787–1810* (National Maritime Museum, Greenwich, 2005).

Russell, Lord, *Knight of the Sword: The Life and Letters of Admiral Sir Sidney William Smith* (Gollancz, 1964).

Smith, Edward, *The Life of Sir Joseph Banks* (John Lane, the Bodley Head, 1911).

Sparrow, Elizabeth, *Secret Service: British Agents in France, 1792–1815* (Woodbridge, 1999).

Sugden, John, *Nelson: A Dream of Glory* (Pimlico, 2004).

———, *Nelson: The Sword of Albion* (The Bodley Head, 2012).

Tolstoy, Nikolai, *The Half-Mad Lord* (Holt, Rinehart, and Winston, 1979).

Weber, David J., *The Spanish Frontier in North America: The Brief Edition* (Yale University Press, 2009).

Williams, Glyn, *Voyages of Delusion* (Harper Collins, 2003).

Printed in Great Britain
by Amazon